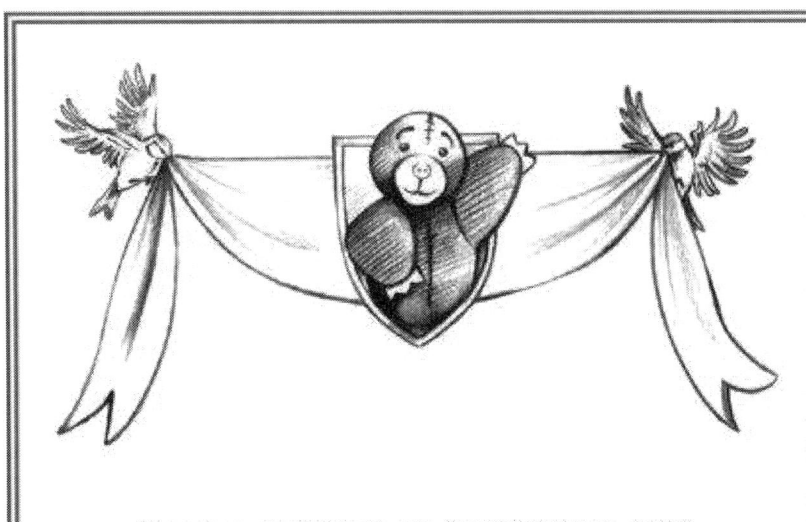

THIS BOOK BELONGS TO

....

....

MOLEY
AND THE
MYSTERIOUS
SEA TURTLES

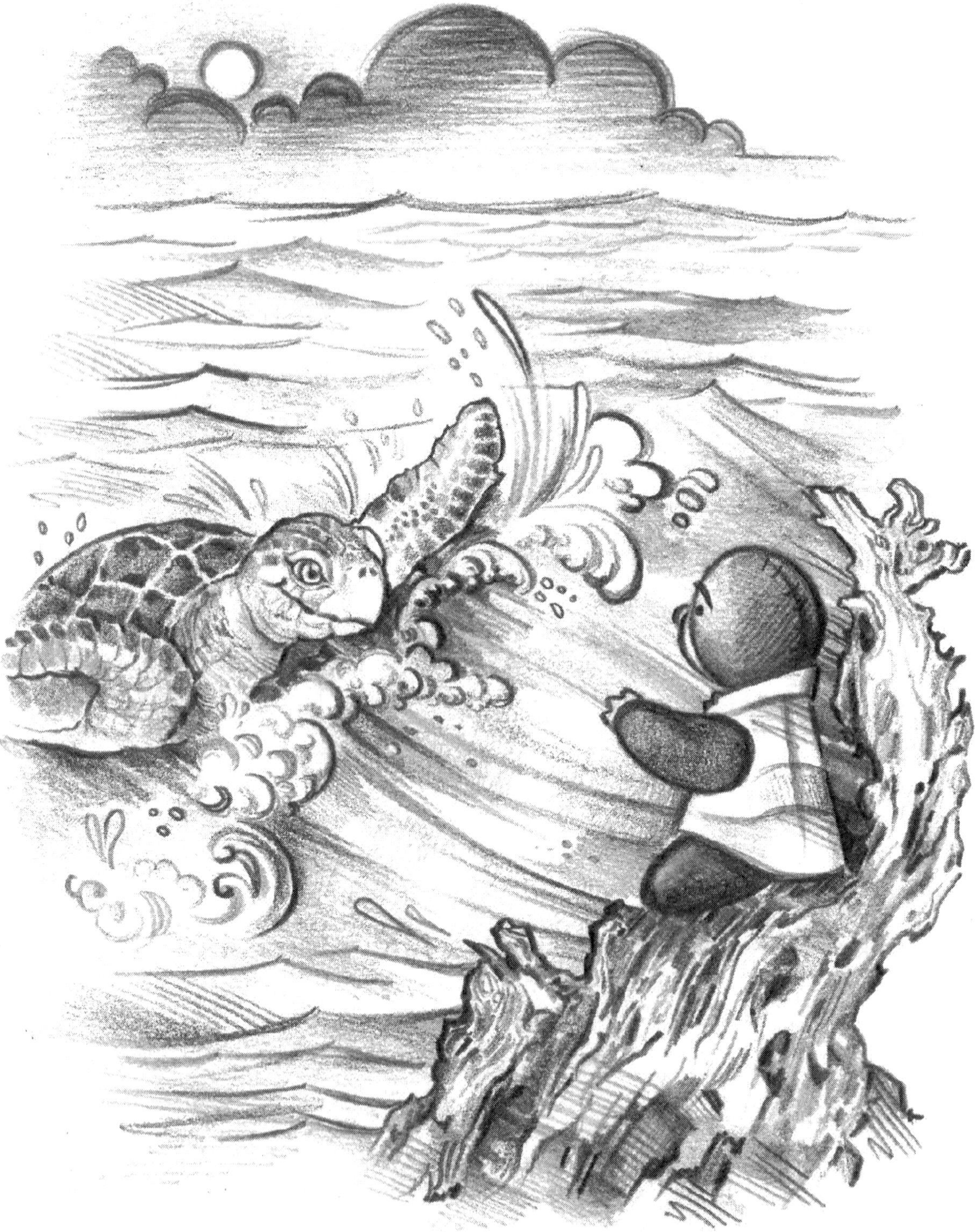

Julia B. Grantham

MOLEY
AND THE MYSTERIOUS SEA TURTLES

Illustrated by
CAROL WELLART

First published in paperback by SDS Media LLP in 2023

ISBN: 9798867012250

Text copyright © Julia Budnik Grantham 2023
Illustrations copyright © Karolina Wellartova 2023
Cover design © Karolina Wellartova, J.BGrantham, Elena Tarnovskaya, 2023

The author and illustrator assert the moral right to be identified
as the author and illustrator of the work.
A CIP catalogue record for this title is available from the British Library.
All rights reserved.
No part of this publication may be reproduced, stored in a retrieval system or transmitted in any form
or by any means, electronic, mechanical, photocopying, recording or otherwise, without the prior
permission of SDS Media LLP.

To Moley's first readers:

The students of

Richmond Elementary School, Rhode Island

and

Freedom Elementary, Florida

OTHER BOOKS ABOUT MOLEY

BY J.B. GRANTHAM

A Mole Like No Other

Also

A Mole Like No Other
Audiobook
Read by Alison Larkin

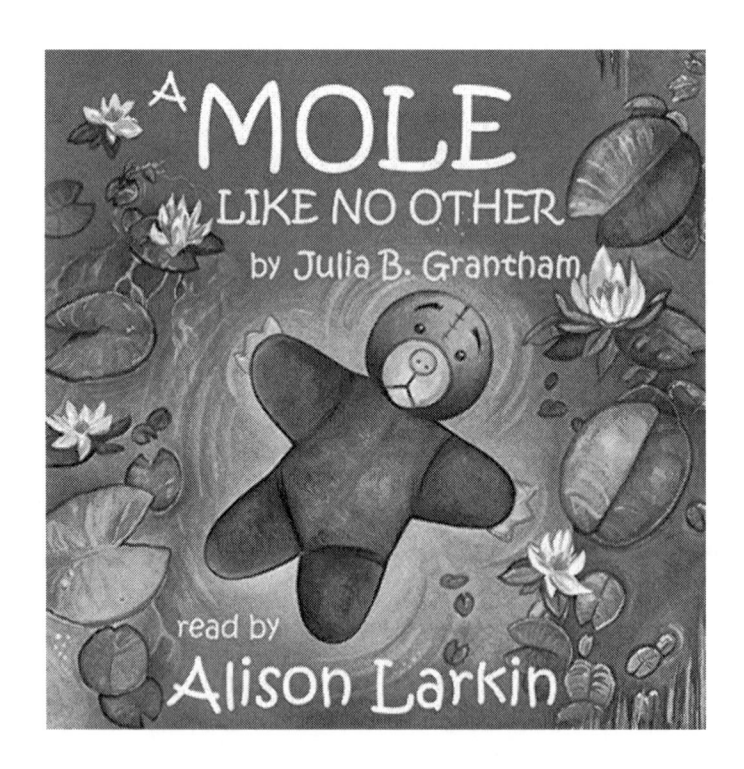

Contents

Chapter One *Moley's on the Move* 11

Chapter Two *Trust the Experts* 20

Chapter Three *Moley's in the Air* 28

Chapter Four *On the Way to Tortuga Key* 35

Chapter Five *The Turtle Watch* 43

Chapter Six *A Pop-Up Tent* 50

Chapter Seven *A Crocodile and an Alligator* 55

Chapter Eight *Twick and a Squabbling Squadron* 62

Chapter Nine *Moley's Days and Nights* 72

Chapter Ten *A Creature in Distress* 78

Chapter Eleven *Endangered Species* 87

Chapter Twelve *Brad the Crab* 91

Chapter Thirteen *A Brazilian Free Tailed Bat* 96

Chapter Fourteen *Operation 'Nest'* 103

Chapter Fifteen *Moley Can't Catch a Break* 113

Chapter Sixteen *The Mysterious Flying Dot* 119

Epilogue 126

More about Moley 133

Readers' Reviews 136

Acknowledgements 140

About the Author 142

About the Illustrator 143

Chapter One

Moley's on the Move

Moley was a mole with a secret.

A toy mole with a secret.

He was a toy mole who could think and talk, jump and walk, and do all the other things that you don't usually expect toy moles to do.

Furthermore, around him all the other animals and toys could do all these things as well!

But – and here comes the secret – they were not allowed to let their humans know that they could do any of it. No talking, no walking and no jumping when people could see them.

Thinking, on the other hand, was not forbidden, even around humans. For thinking is the very thing that no one can forbid,

And today Moley had a lot of thinking to do. And quick thinking too!

For Moley was the kind of mole who always felt responsible for everyone and everything around him. He liked to make sure that everyone knew what they were doing and everything was clearly explained.

But...

Today Moley had to leave home very suddenly. He was picked up by his owner, a boy called Ashley, to go on holiday with him and his parents, Mr and Mrs Richards, who Moley often called Dad and Mum, or even Daddy and Mummy, just like Ashley did. Their departure was so swift that Moley hadn't had a chance to talk to his friends about any arrangements that had to be put in place while he was away.

How would they manage all their duties without him?

And the duties were great indeed!

For the last three weeks, Ashley's toys – the owl, called Owlie; Boris, the Bear; two dogs, Rosie and Rusty; and the dinosaurs, Dina and Bronti – had all taken upon themselves the responsibility of protecting a family of ducks from the dangers of the night.

The duck family consisted of a father, Ludwig, a mother, Alexis, and six little ducklings, including the one Moley had saved in a big storm, who was named after him – Moley-Two. This little family was in constant danger from the animals that hunt at night, called 'the predators', because Ludwig and Alexis, just like all living creatures, had to sleep at night, and the predators could sneak up on their babies unexpectedly.

Luckily, the toys – Moley and his friends – didn't *need* to sleep, because they were toys (they could sleep, but only if they chose to) and, therefore, they were able to keep watch over the ducks at night.

Moley had developed a timetable according to which all the toy animals, except Boris, who was too big to get outside through the cat-flap, guarded the ducklings every night in pairs, and it worked very well. No predators had managed to attack them since the watch began.

But now, with Moley gone, how would this timetable work?

Owlie, whom Moley was paired with, would not have a companion. What would she do?

Moley was really worried.

The only comfort he could think of were the parting words Gordon the Pigeon said to him as the Richards' car was about to drive away from the house:

"Moley! You've done everything you could to ensure everyone's

safety. The toys and animals are all working together and helping each other. You can go with Ashley and enjoy your trip. You deserve it. All will be well."

'All will be well,' Moley repeated in his head Gordon's words and felt reassured a little.

But still, for the first few minutes of his car journey all his thoughts were with the worries he'd left behind.

Yet... as it often happens, the further Moley got from home, the more his thoughts turned to the future.

By the time the Richards' car left the country road and joined another – so wide that vehicles rushed along it four abreast in both directions – Moley's mind was firmly focused on the world around him. Because it was fascinating in the extreme!

He had only just got used to the widest road he'd ever seen – Ashley called it a *motorway* – when their car arrived at a building filled in all directions with other cars.

Mr Richards drove up the slopy spiral ramp from one floor to another, higher and higher, but each floor was packed with vehicles, standing tightly in many rows. Finally, when Moley had started to worry that they would never stop this endless drive, Ashley spotted a gap between two cars.

Mr Richards neatly inserted their car between two others, and they squeezed themselves out, picked their suitcases from the boot and marched towards a massive building.

Moley didn't know that there were such gigantic structures in the world. He'd always imagined that their house was big. But now he realised how wrong he was!

This new building had high ceilings and vast spacious halls, filled with people rushing by, paying no attention to their little group.

"We are at the airport," Ashley told Moley, kindly remembering that it was Moley's first visit to such a place.

The Richards family joined a long queue that snaked towards a row of counters with a big sign above them that Moley just about managed to read. BAG DROP, it said, which made Moley feel very uneasy.

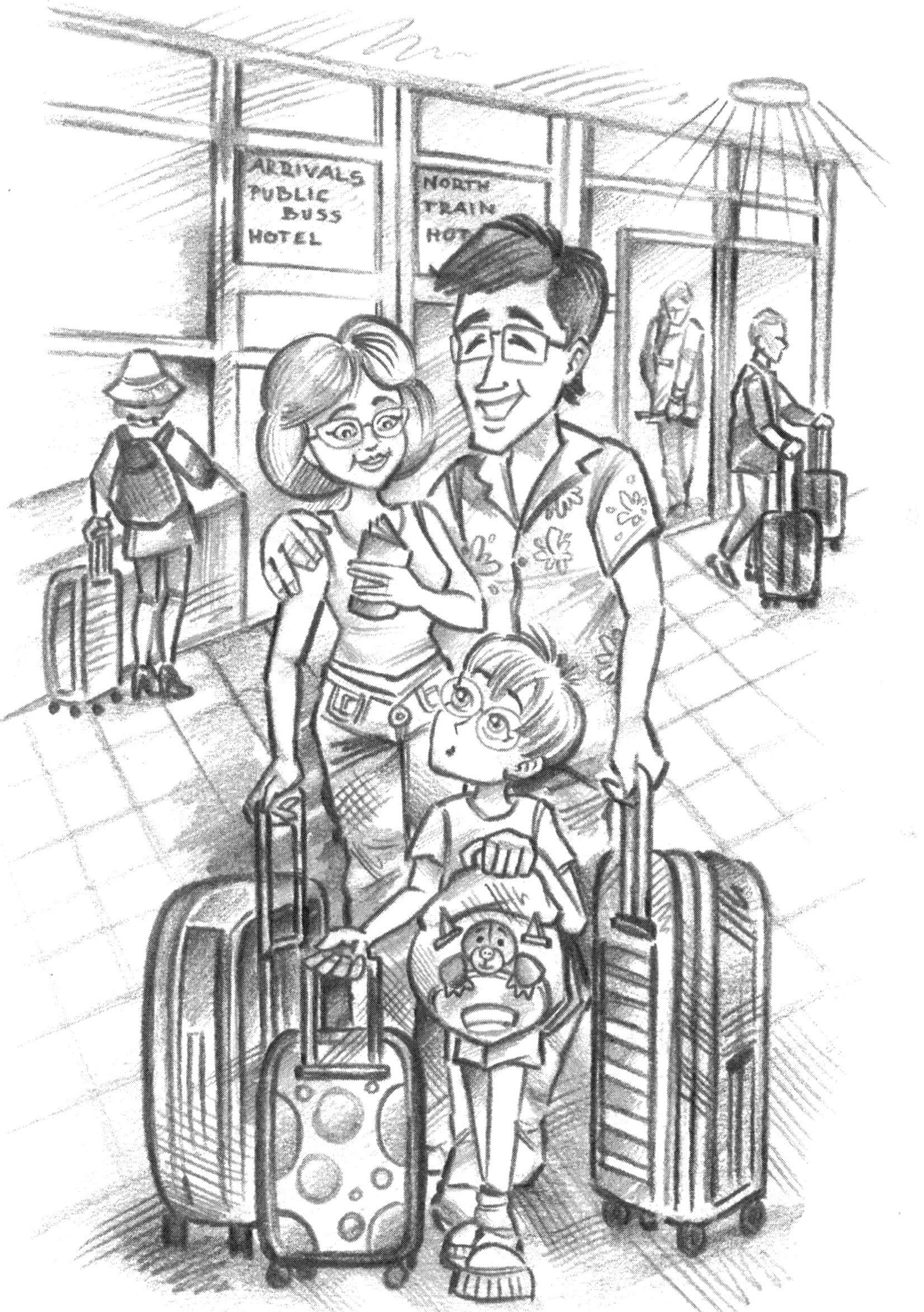
ARRIVALS
PUBLIC
BUSS
HOTEL
NORTH
TRAIN

He was in Ashley's backpack, which was technically, a bag. But he didn't want to be dropped. Didn't want that at all.

He stretched his neck as far as he could (not very far!), trying to see what was happening at the mysterious bag drop. To his horror he saw that people were placing their bags onto a wide belt that then carried the bags away. He couldn't see where, but he was sure to some sort of cliff edge!

'Oh, no!' exclaimed Moley inwardly. 'I don't want to be dropped!"

What options did he have?

He could jump out of the backpack and get lost, but he loved Ashley and loved his family and friends. He didn't want to lose them!

He could hold on to Ashley and not go with the bag to the drop, but he was not allowed to betray his secret, and show the humans that he not just a toy, that he was alive, could move and talk, and understand.

What could he do?

The moving belt was getting nearer, and Moley was getting more anxious by the moment, until, suddenly, a very bright thought occurred to him.

'I love Ashley, but Ashley loves me too! He will not allow someone he loves to drop over a cliff edge! I should trust him!'

With this resolution in mind, Moley sighed deeply and looked ahead with hope.

The Richards family reached the counter and started putting their luggage onto the moving belt. Mum's suitcase, Dad's suitcase, Ashley's suitcase...

Moley held his breath.

"This is my hand luggage," said Ashley to an official looking lady at the counter, showing her his backpack, with Moley sticking out.

"No problem," said the lady, without a second look, and attached a band to the backpack's handle that said APPROVED.

Moley could finally breathe out!

He loved the new band – it meant that he and his bag were approved by the official lady and nothing could stop them from going on holiday with Ashley.

Little did he know that there were other obstacles to go through!

Chapter Two

Trust the Experts

Next, they travelled up the moving stairs.

If he were by himself, Moley, probably, would not have dared to put a foot on them – ever!

But he was in the rucksack that was on Ashley's back, and, as such, had very little choice about using or not using the moving stairs. Ashley didn't seem to be bothered by them at all – he stepped onto the staircase that moved on its own without any fear.

'I can trust him completely,' thought Moley. 'He knows what he is doing.'

Then they went through the gates that open and close by themselves when you show them a piece of paper.

It seemed that most things at the airport worked by themselves, as if by magic!

At last, they reached the stop that Ashley called 'security'.

Mr and Mrs Richards and Ashley all stood by another counter with trays moving along it on a belt. Moving belts did not surprise Moley anymore, he'd seen plenty of them today. He was APPROVED and didn't expect to go on the belt.

He was wrong!

Ashley put his rucksack into one of the trays on the belt, and – what Moley didn't expect at all! – pushed him inside and fastened the zip.

And all at a time when Moley had just decided to trust him completely!

Moley was in the dark. He felt betrayed and panicky.

Mustering his wits, he tried to focus on his sensations. There was movement underneath, his tray was sliding towards an unknown destination. Desperately wanting to know what was going on, Moley wiggled in the bag, trying to undo the zip above his head, to see where he was being taken. He managed to create a tiny crack in the fastening just as he felt the rucksack lifted into the air and a loud male voice calling:

"Whose bag is this?"

"Mine," Moley heard Ashley responding. "It's mine."

"We need to open it and check," said the man, severely.

"But what is the matter?" this was Mr Richards's voice.

"There seems to be a live animal in this bag," came the reply. "My colleague, Officer Perkins, detected some movement."

"Live animal?!" exclaimed Mr Richards. "Preposterous!"

"We need to check," the man insisted.

Moley heard the sound of a zip opening and saw the light of day again. He froze, as he always did when people were around, staring earnestly at the world with his unblinking small eyes.

"It's only Moley," said Ashley. "He is my friend, but he is a toy."

"Hm…" said another man who'd come over and looked puzzled. "Let's check the rest of the bag."

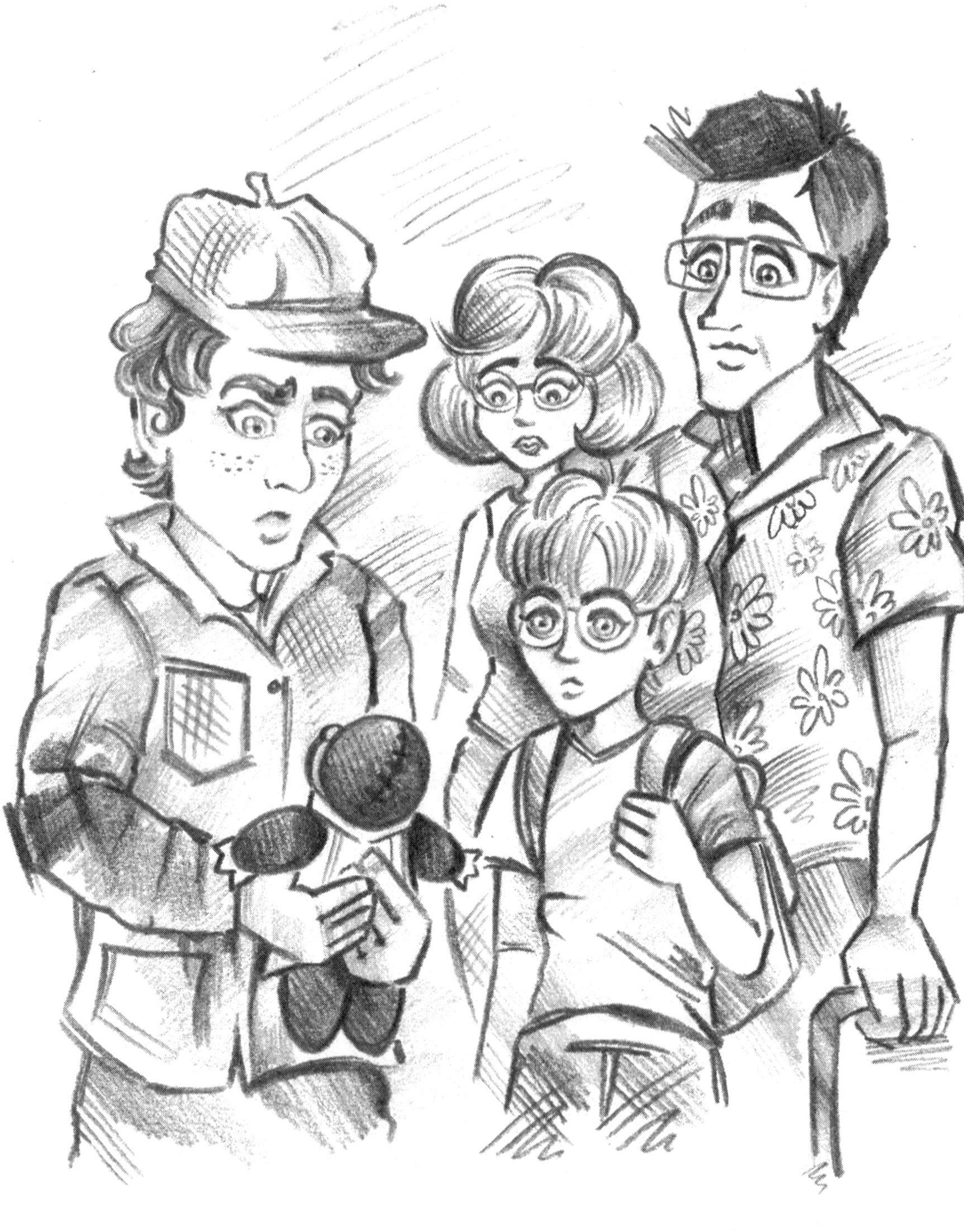

The contents of Ashley's bag were placed on the table and checked carefully, but, of course, no animal was found.

Moley figured out that his attempts to open the zip had somehow been noticed by one of the security guards – but how? He was inside the bag! How could the guard have seen him? Could this man see through things?

Meanwhile the security guard put all the contents of Ashley's rucksack back inside, until only Moley was left on the table.

"Perkins!" called the guard, and a young officer moved in their direction, looking a bit embarrassed.

"Is this the animal you spotted in the bag?" the guard asked, passing Moley to young Perkins.

The young man's face went pink and his ears – scarlet.

"It really moved," he said.

The older officer smirked:

"It's no surprise, I guess. You're still of an age when one believes that toys are alive and the tooth fairy gives you money."

'That's not a nice thing to say," said Mr Richards to the older guard.

And Mrs Richards said to a very embarrassed Perkins:

"It's ok, Mr Perkins. Better safe than sorry. You were right to make sure."

She offered him her hand and he shook it gratefully, returning Moley to her.

The Richardses turned around and walked away, Moley still in Mrs Richards' hand.

"You've learned about X-ray machines today, Moley," she said to him. "Better stay still when you're inside one," she added with a wink and gently pushed him back to the top of Ashley's backpack.

Mummy always seemed to understand more things about Moley than other people did!

Moley was quite shaken by the incident. He realised that he'd almost got Ashley into trouble and felt very ashamed. He also was sorry for young Perkins, because he knew that Perkins had told the truth about seeing something moving inside the bag.

He didn't know what X-ray machines were, but guessed that they helped security people to look inside the bags. Moley made a mental note to himself to tell Owlie about these machines when he saw her again, she loved this sort of clever thing, and felt a wave of sadness in his heart – Owlie and all his friends suddenly felt so far away!

When was he going to see them again?

The area they moved into now was a feast for all senses: it had shops as far as the eye could see, filled with a myriad of shiny, glittering and fragrant things - perfumes, chocolates and toys. Loud speakers were making announcements; bright screens blinked in many colours, showing long lists of destinations.

The Richards stopped by one of these screens.

"There!" shouted Ashley, pointing at the screen. "Look, Tampa!"

Moley didn't know what Tampa was but he liked the sound of it. The word felt dynamic like 'tempo', and spiritual, like 'temple'. It was a good place to travel to.

The family rushed in the direction of the gate listed on the screen. They walked and walked and walked, along the endless corridors, and for a moment Moley got worried that they were going to walk all the way to Tampa.

But, thank goodness, the corridors finally came to an end, and the family joined yet another long queue of people, all facing towards a screen with the words TAMPA – NOW BOARDING on it.

Have you ever been on a plane?

Moley hadn't.

He knew *of* planes, of course, he'd seen their pictures in books, on Mr Richards' laptop and on TV, but deep in his soul he'd always had doubts that these huge machines could actually fly in the sky.

His doubts now resurfaced, especially when he spotted through the floor-to-ceiling window the plane they were about to board.

The plane looked like a blue whale. At least that's how Moley imagined a blue whale might look. It was gigantic! As tall as it was wide, it had a hump on the top with a small window at the front. The rest of its body had lots and lots of tiny windows, lined up neatly in a row. Moley tried counting them, but quickly gave up, as he could only count to ten and there were *many* more than ten tiny windows.

'How is this thing going to fly?' Moley asked himself. 'It must be so heavy – it might not even move!'

This thought gave him hope. Maybe they would get into the plane, but with all of them on board, it *would be* too heavy to move and they'd all go back home.

How longingly he thought of Ashley's bedroom with its soft wide bed, and comfortable window sills to safely observe the world outside; and of his friends – Owlie and Boris, Rusty and Rosie, Bronti and Dina, Ludwig, Alexis and Gordon in the garden, and all the ducklings, especially – Moley-TWO. Why did he want to travel? Why couldn't he stay at home with his friends?!?

The panic was overwhelming and Moley didn't like it.

'Stop,' he said to himself. 'This won't do! These thoughts are in your head, but how do you know that they are true? Look around, what do you see?'

He looked, and he saw people who weren't panicking.

He saw children smiling and laughing, jumping in anticipation, pulling impatiently at their parents' hands.

He saw grown-ups chatting excitedly, discussing plans for their holiday.

He saw Mr and Mrs Richards beaming at each other, and heard them saying: "Can't wait."

He saw Ashley, his nose in a book called 'Florida', waiting patiently in the queue, not a worry on his face.

'Right, Moley,' our mole said to himself. 'See? No one else is panicking. You might think these people are silly and they don't understand. But you know that Mummy and Daddy, at least, are terribly clever, and understand everything. And they are calm. Ashley is clever too. And he is calm. You need to calm down as well.'

And at that moment he heard in his head the voice of his friend Gordon, the pigeon, who'd once said: 'Trust the experts.'

'Exactly!' thought Moley and instead of panicking he decided to trust the people around him and try to enjoy his new adventure.

Chapter Three

Moley's in the Air

Soon they walked through a long narrow tube that brought them straight to the plane's door.

A very friendly young man smiled at all of them and said: "Welcome aboard."

Inside, the plane looked even bigger than outside. It had two narrow aisles running along its length, so long that Moley couldn't see where they started and where they ended.

The seats were lined in rows – and Moley managed to count them – three on the side, four in the middle – three on the other side. It took him a while to put these numbers together.

Can *you* do it?

I'll leave here some space for you to figure it out and then you can check whether it is the same answer that Moley got!

After much mental effort he came up with an answer –

TEN!

The Richards took three seats on the side – Ashley squeezed himself into the seat by the window, Mrs Richards next to him and Mr Richards – by the aisle.

Ashley took his rucksack off his back, and pushed it under the seat in front of him, taking out Moley and his Florida book first. He placed Moley on the armrest of his seat in such a way that the mole could see out of the window, as well as inside the aircraft.

Moley devised a good tactic that allowed him to look in either direction. He could look out of the window if he closed his right eye, and inside the plane if he closed his left. As you know, Moley's eyes were tiny and set deep inside his thick fur, so nobody would have noticed him closing one eye or another from time to time.

Boarding the plane took a long time – people kept coming and coming, and it seemed that they would never end, but everything eventually ends, if you wait patiently.

Finally, all the passengers occupied their seats and, all of a sudden, the back of the one in front of Ashley lit up and became a TV screen.

A pretty and very smiley young lady on the screen said yet another "Welcome aboard" and asked everyone to pay attention to the 'safety on board' video.

Moley always took safety VERY seriously, so he opened both eyes and kept them peeled at the screen. So did Ashley. They listened carefully about the exits, and the seat belts, and the oxygen masks, and the life jackets.

Moley found everything clear and reassuring, apart from one thing...

There wasn't a seatbelt for him.

It had evidently crossed Ashley's mind too, because after the safety announcement he took Moley and placed him into the pocket under the screen, legs – in the bag, head and paws – free, with a tight grip across his belly, holding him securely in place.

'Excellent,' thought Moley, feeling very grateful, that his Ashley was so inventive.

Ready to fly, Moley gazed around and listened to all the announcements until the engines started to roar and then he showed weakness and closed his eyes. The roar intensified and the plane started moving, slowly at first, then faster and faster, and then so fast that Moley's eyes sprang open despite his fear.

And he saw it!

The airport building in the window was running away from him and then – dropped out of sight.

'We are flying!' thought Moley. He wanted to shout it out loud, but caught himself in time, and only whispered in the smallest voice possible:

"We are flying!"

And no one could hear him over the noise of the engines.

The lift-off was very quick, and soon the speakers pinged and Ashley said: 'The seatbelt sign is off, you can come out of your safety place, Mols'.

He pulled Moley out of the pocket and placed him by the window again, so he could see everything.

Moley could see the green and yellow patchwork of fields underneath, that looked very similar to Ashley's bedspread, the glittering mirrors of lakes and ponds, the thin grey lines of roads with tiny ants of cars running along them.

Somewhere down there was his pond, too. With Ludwig and Alexis probably looking into the sky, their heads bent sideways, following with their eyes the small bird of a plane, spreading its wings over their little family, their garden, their whole precious green world.

"Bye, bye home, I'll see you soon," Moley whispered under his breath.

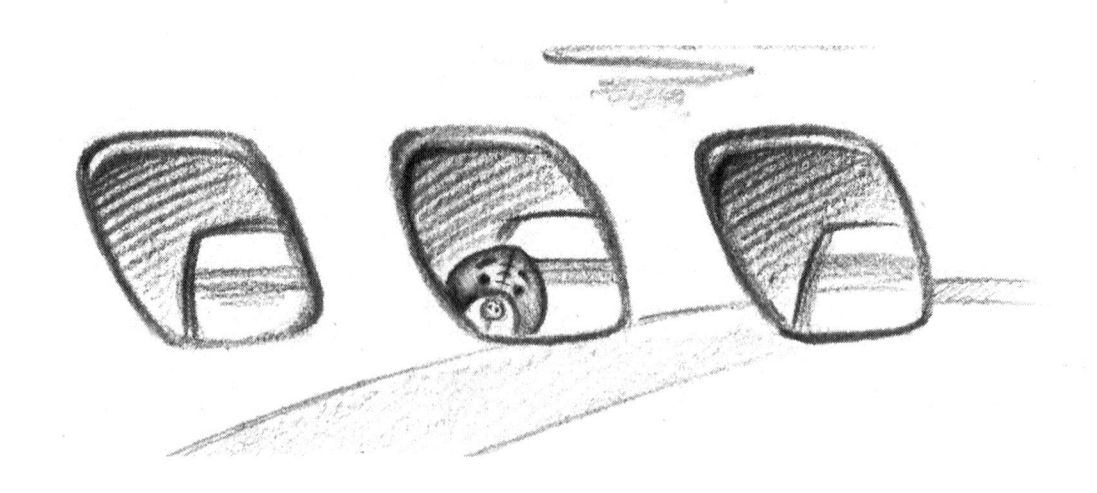

He noticed that his fears had disappeared. He was too excited to be scared.

The plane kept going up, and now, as far as Moley's eyes could see, the world was covered in something white. It looked like an enormous plate of whipped cream, or like a huge bubble bath covered in thick foam – white, fluffy and inviting. Moley thought how lovely it would be to dive head first into this soft fluffiness and immediately felt a bit ashamed – for he knew enough to understand that these were clouds and he could fall right through, if he decided to dive into them.

When the clouds eventually parted, he saw the endless shiny water surface far below.

"It's the Atlantic Ocean," said Ashley, "We are flying to America."

The flight was long. Ashley read his book, ate two big meals, watched three films on flight TV and even had a little sleep.

Moley continued looking out of his window.

A voice was sounding in his head that went like this:

'Don't waste your time, Moley. Don't look away. Pay attention to every moment of this wonderful day. You are a little toy mole, who spent years collecting dust under the bed, and then – more years inside a stuffy box, with a yellow tractor pressed into your chest. You were bought at a school fair for a pound and started a new life with your new family and many friends. And now, you – the very same mole – are flying above the clouds over the Atlantic Ocean, to a new place called America. Don't sleep or look away – pay attention, notice every little thing about this journey and store it safely in your mind forever.'

After several hours the sound system did another ping and the captain of the plane announced: 'We are about to start our descent to the airport of Tampa. Please fasten your seatbelts.'.

Ashley placed Moley into his pocket at the back of the seat in front and clicked the buckle of his seatbelt. They were ready for landing.

Chapter Four

On the Way to Tortuga Key

Once back on firm land, Mr and Mrs Richards and Asley collected their luggage (their suitcases came amongst hundreds of others on a long circular moving belt), picked up a car they'd rented and, putting the directions into Dad's phone, set off towards their final destination.

Moley looked out of the window, marvelling at all the things he saw. Everything seemed different. The sky was higher and even bluer than at home. The clouds stood like great towers – tall, massive and blindingly white. The sea was turquoise blue and stretched as far as the eye could see.

But the most remarkable part of the journey for Moley was crossing a huge bridge. At first Moley couldn't understand, what was the strange structure he saw in the distance? Everyone in the car got excited about it and started talking at once:

"Look, it's the Skyway!"

"The Skyway? What do you mean?"

"It's the name of the bridge – the Sunshine Skyway Bridge."

"It is amazing! So tall!"

"It's huge!"

"It's magnificent!"

Indeed, it was an imposing construction! Thick yellow cables held up the road that rose into the sky so steeply it seemed cut off at the top.

Moley was about to start worrying and whether the road continued on the other side, or whether they'd just drop off, bags and all, but he reminded himself of his newly found resolution to trust the experts.

Mr Richards was the expert in this situation, he was driving calmly and confidently, so Moley relaxed and enjoyed the beautiful views of the endless sea on both sides of the bridge.

The ride wasn't too long and after passing many tall buildings and traffic lights, the car crossed another, much smaller, bridge that clanked metallically under the wheels, and turned into a road with neat houses and flower bushes on both sides.

A large sign stood on the side of the road.

It showed a beach, surrounded by palm trees, a large umbrella and some footprints in the sand, and big letters, which Ashley immediately read:

"Welcome to Tortuga Key."

"Do you know what it means, Ashley?" asked Mr Richards.

"Well, I know Tortuga," said Ashley slightly frowning, "I think, it means a 'sea turtle', right?"

"Correct," said Dad.

"Key though," continued Ashley, "I, obviously, know what 'key' means, but it seems different here."

He looked confused.

"Yep," said Mr Richards. "Key means 'a little island' here. It comes from Spanish. They borrowed the word."

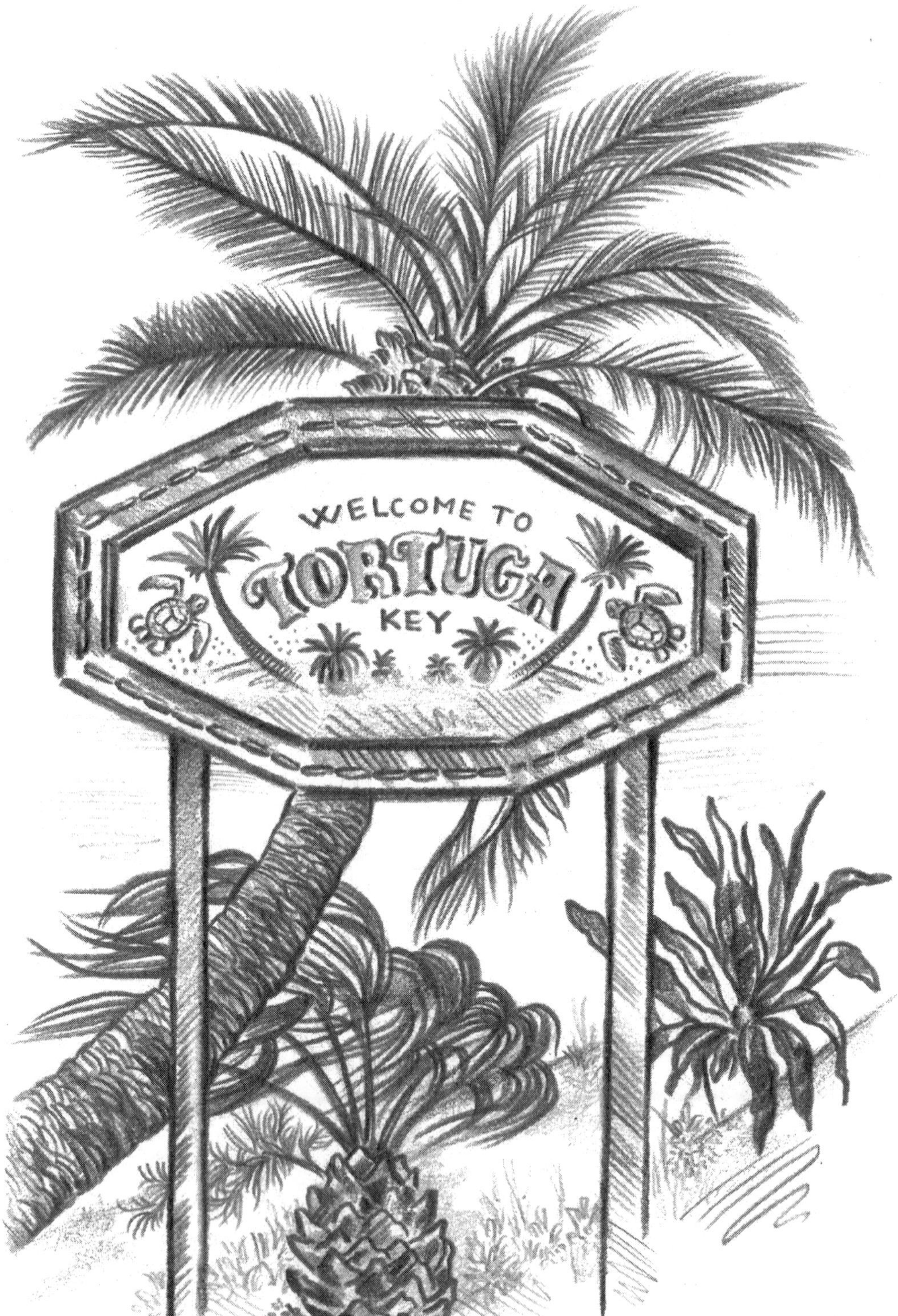
WELCOME TO
TORTUGA
KEY

"So, it says 'Welcome to a Sea Turtle Island', right?" asked Ashley.

"Exactly!" said Dad. "And – if we are lucky, we will see some sea turtles. They are not easy to find in the wild."

Moley really wanted to know what these 'sea turtles' were. He had no idea how they looked and what they did, and why they were not easy to find. But Ashley's attention was caught by something else now.

Bright, tidy houses appeared on each side, with strange colourful sculptures by the side of the road in front of each of them.

"These are letterboxes," explained Mr Richards. "They call them 'mailboxes' here".

There were many mailboxes of different shapes.

Some looked like human figures, others – like animals, and Ashley happily named them:

Flamingo!

Crocodile!

Some were shaped like creatures unknown to Moley, and he hoped that one of them might turn out to be the mysterious sea turtle, that gave the island its name, but as Ashley continued, there was no luck:

Seahorse!

Dolphin!

Hippopotamus!

"Eh, no," said Dad. "That isn't a hippo. It's a manatee. See, it's got a tail like a seal?"

'Wow!' thought Moley. 'There were so many animals he'd never even heard of.'

His desire to learn all the new names and meet all these new animals made him even more excited.

This holiday was going to be epic!

The place they finally stopped at was a series of two-storey building stretching along the beach in a wide semi-circle.

The buildings were divided into many apartments. Mr Richards called them 'condominiums', Mrs Richards, 'condos'. Moley much preferred 'condominiums', for, as you might remember, our mole always had a soft spot for long words and would never use a short word where a long one would do.

So, the building was divided into many condominiums, all facing the sea.

The Richards' condo was the last one on the ground floor, closest to the sea, and when they entered it, they saw the wide, floor-to-ceiling glass door that led from the lounge to a terrace that took them right onto the sandy beach.

"Oh, wow!" shouted Ashley.

He slid the glass door open and ran out, leaving his backpack, with Moley in it, indoors.

'Well, thank you very much, Ashley,' thought Moley sarcastically. 'Leave me behind, when all the interesting things are about to happen!'

But Ashley was back soon and took his backpack and his suitcase into his holiday bedroom to unpack.

The bedroom was small, but perfectly situated – its window looked right onto the beach.

It had two single beds, a chest of drawers, and a wardrobe.

"All you need for happiness," commented Ashley, taking Moley out of the backpack and placing him on the pillow of the bed next to the wardrobe.

"This will be your bed, Moley, I'll sleep on the one next to the window."

Then Ashley put his suitcase onto Moley's bed and unzipped it. He took out all his clothes and quickly put them away. He left other things in the case, leaving it open. Moley didn't mind. He only needed a very little room, and was happy to share his bed with Ashley's suitcase.

At this point Mummy called Ashley to eat and after that everyone went to sleep, having a well-deserved rest after a very long day.

Chapter Five

The Turtle Watch

Next morning, Ashley was up when it was still dark.

It wasn't surprising, as Florida time is five hours behind England's, where Ashley came from.

Can you figure out what time it would be in England when it is five in the morning in Florida?

As soon as his eyes opened, Ashley jumped out of bed, picked up Moley, tiptoed through the lounge and sneaked onto the beach through the sliding door.

It was very warm. The sky above was still dark, but on the left, far away above the sea, Moley noticed a narrow pink ribbon that was getting wider and paler by the moment, with a hint of yellow and white where it touched the sea.

The beach was endless. It stretched all the way to the horizon along the sea edge in both directions. The sand looked soft and Moley couldn't wait until Ashley would let him down on the ground so that he could sink his wide paws into it.

Ashley walked with Moley to the sea edge and put his feet into the water.

"Wow!" he said. "It's really warm! Warmer than the air!"

Moley was happy to take his word for it. Ever since his adventure just a few weeks ago back home, when he was accidently thrown into the pond by Alexis, the Mother Duck, and very nearly drowned, he wasn't too keen on water.

Ashley strolled along the sea, softly splashing water with his feet. It was incredibly peaceful. It seemed to Moley that at that moment he and Ashley were alone in the world, two souls by the wide dark sea.

However, before long, he was proven wrong, when he spotted a group of people in the distance. Ashley noticed them too.

"Do you see them, Moley?" he said in a hushed voice. "Shall we go towards them or away from them?"

Moley was all for going towards them, but he wasn't allowed to say it, for he was a toy, so Ashley had to make a decision himself. He moved tentatively in the people's direction.

The strangers were grouped together over something that looked like a pile of sand. They were pushing long yellow sticks into the sand around the pile and stretched bright orange tape between the sticks, so that the pile of sand was surrounded by a barrier of sorts on all sides.

Soon they noticed Ashley, with Moley in his hand – there were no other people on the beach.

"Hey there," called out a woman with a broad smile on a friendly face.

The other three people looked at Ashley and Moley with curious, but inviting expressions.

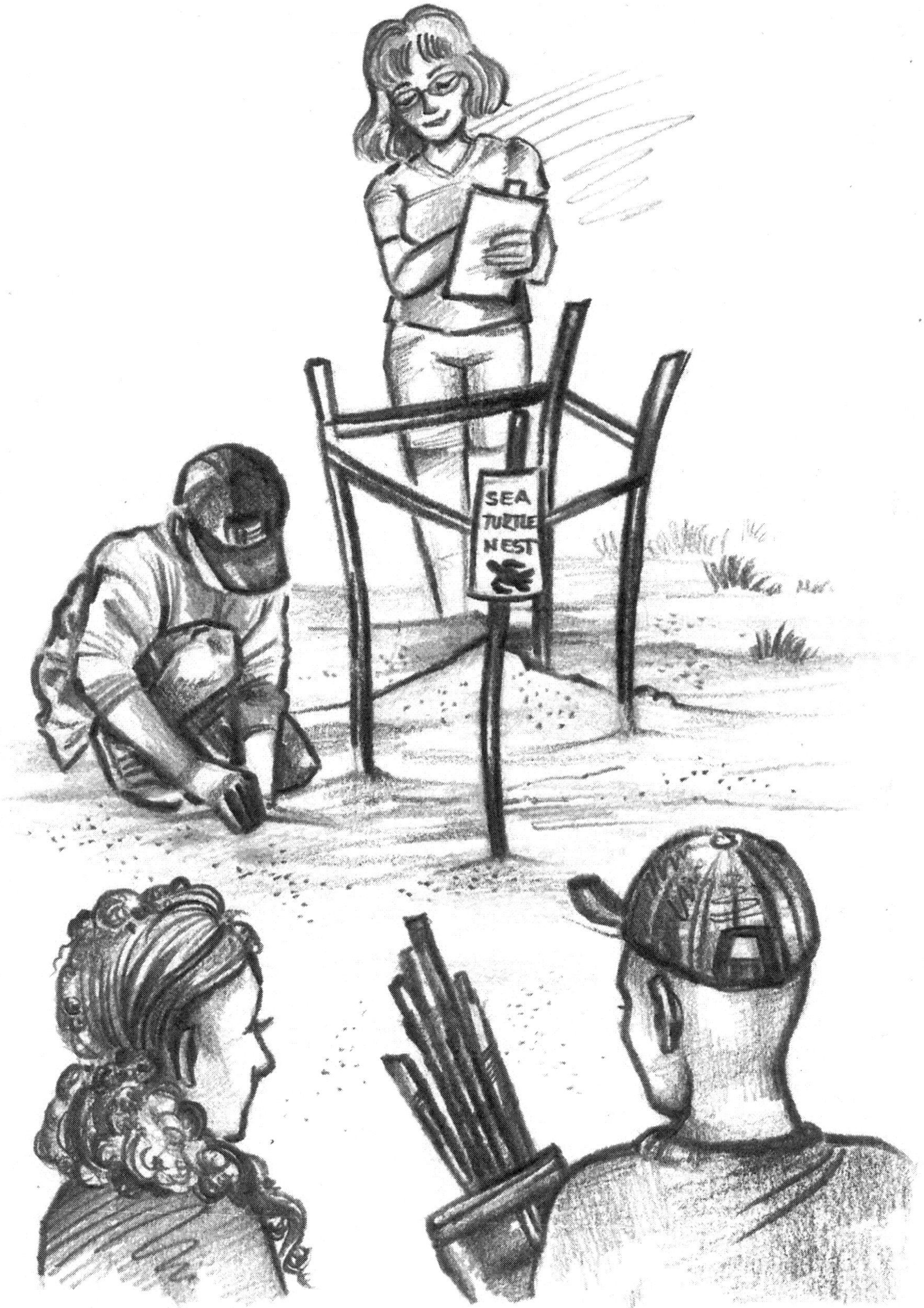
SEA
TURTLE
NEST

They were all wearing blue T-shirts with big letters printed on the front, that said TORTUGA KEY TURTLE WATCH.

"Hello," said Ashley. "We're on holiday here and I couldn't sleep."

"Sure," the friendly woman answered. "Do you want to know what we're doing?"

"Yes, please," said Ashley, eagerly.

"You see, we are the Turtle Watch'. You know what turtles are?"

"Of course," said Ashley.

Moley wished Ashley didn't know, for Moley didn't have the foggiest.

"This beach is very popular with turtles," continued the young woman. "But it's popular with people too, and our job is to make sure that the turtles and the humans coexist harmoniously."

'Turtles and humans coexist harmoniously,' repeated Moley in his head. He liked these people.

"Look here," called a man with a shaved head. "Can you see this track? Looks like a tractor went across the beach and right into the ocean, doesn't it?"

Ashley and Moley both had a look and, indeed, saw strange markings in the sand. It was a wide track, or rather two parallel tracks, that looked nothing like anything Moley had seen before. The man called it 'like a tractor', but Moley couldn't say he knew how a tractor's track would look, so this description didn't help him.

The man, meanwhile, continued:

"An adult sea turtle comes out of the water at night and goes across the beach to find a spot for her nest. Then she digs the sand with her back flippers. Deep, sometimes as deep as two feet, and then she lays her eggs, up to a hundred eggs at a time."

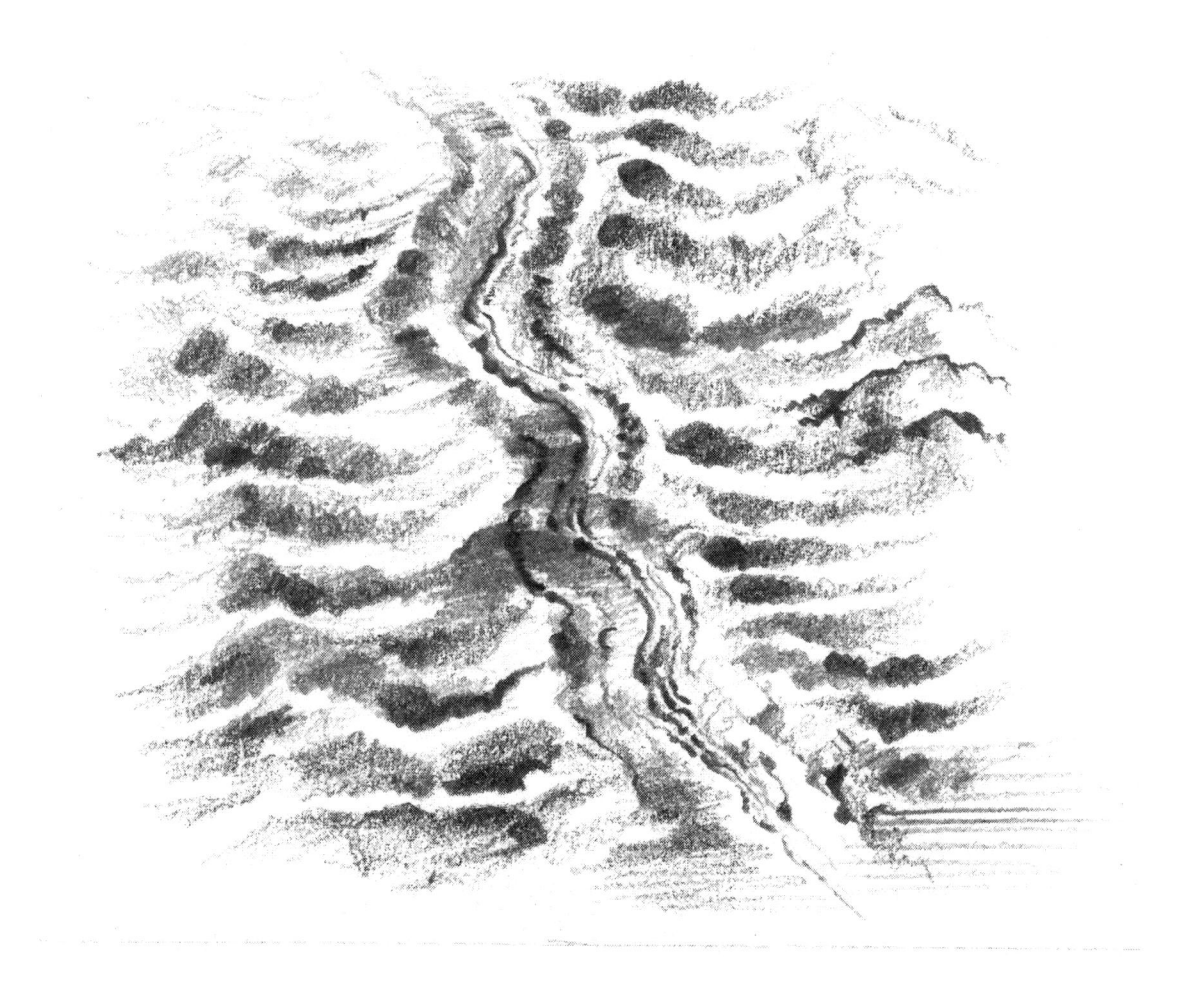

"A hundred!" exclaimed Ashley with astonishment, echoing Moley's thoughts.

"Yes, then she fills the nest with sand and goes back to the sea, leaving just this slightly raised sand hill. Do you see what might be the problem?"

Ashley furrowed his brow, he really wanted to answer correctly:

"If it's not easy to spot the nest," he said, "when people come in the morning, they might accidentally disturb it."

"Well done!" exclaimed the man, and the woman who'd spoken before high-fived Ashley, beaming at him. "People might place their sun beds onto the nests, or stick the poles of their beach umbrellas into them or even start building sand castles right on top."

"That is why," added another woman, with glasses and a kindly face, "we patrol the beach every morning before dawn and mark all the new nests, like so."

She pointed to some writing on the yellow pole.

"See, we write here the date we've discovered the nest, calculate the date when the eggs might hatch, and add this information onto the stick too."

Ashley looked satisfied with this information, but Moley's head was popping, full of questions he couldn't ask.

'Hmmm.... this "don't talk around people" business is a real bother,' he thought to himself. 'I have so many questions, but I have to keep my mouth shut! It's not fair!'

The group of turtle watchers was moving along the beach, Ashley and Moley with them. Soon they found another turtle trail that led all the way across the beach into the sandy dunes covered with dry wispy grass, close to the buildings, and there, between two shallow dunes, they found a new nest.

"This one is ok," said a man with a beard, who hadn't spoken until then. "But sometimes they choose really bad places, on paths, or roads, even on building sites. Then we need to excavate the nest and take the eggs into incubators, because they don't have a chance to survive in such places."

At this point they heard Mrs Richards' voice coming over the beach: "Ashley!"

"Oh, it's Mum! She's lost me!" exclaimed Ashley, taking off from the spot. "I'll come back tomorrow!" he shouted, looking back at his new friends.

"See ya!" shouted back the smiley woman, as Ashley with Moley in his hand sped back towards their condo.

***

Ashley was told off.

Not too severely, but firmly.

He was told not to disappear like that from the condo again without warning. He was told not to go on his own and meet strangers, who might be friendly, yes, but also might be dangerous.

Ashley promised, but happily informed his mother and father that he was planning to meet his new friends tomorrow morning at dawn, and asked them not to consider it disappearing, because he'd given them this warning.

"Fair enough," said Mr Richards. "But this time one of us will go with you."

The matter was settled and the first day of holidays rolled on happily – with swimming in the sea (Ashley loved the water – "It's as warm as a bath and tastes of gherkins!" he said to his parents who laughed and agreed), walking along the water's edge, picking up sea shells of different shapes and sizes, and watching the sun set slowly in the evening, colouring the sky in rich vivid colours, from light blue, mellow yellow and soft pink to deep purple, hot orange and flaming red, each moment looking more spectacular than the previous one.

Chapter Six

A Pop-Up Tent

Next morning, once again, just before dawn, Ashley picked up Moley and knocked on his parents' door.

"Who wants to go with me?"

"Ashley… oh no."

They heard moaning voices from behind the door, but a couple of minutes later Mr Richards pulled the door open and emerged from the room, looking rather grumpy.

"Do we have to go so early, Ash?" he said. "I'm on holiday, son…"

"You don't have to go at all, Dad!" said Ashley brightly, but as often happens with grown-ups, this only made Mr Richards more determined to join them. Go figure!

Mr Richards, Ashley and Moley left the condo through the sliding door and walked onto the beach. Soon they spotted the familiar group of turtle watchers in the distance and Ashley ran ahead to greet them.

This time all the formalities were observed, and they started with proper introductions.

Ashley's dad stretched his hand out to each member of the small party in turn, introducing himself by his first name, 'Adam'.

Ashley in turn did the same and soon they all knew each other's names.

The woman with a broad smile was called Monica. The kindly woman with glasses was called Renee. The man with a shaved head – Ron, and the bearded man – Bob.

Even Moley was introduced and shook hands with each of them in turn.

After the introductions they were happy to continue with their explorations and explanations.

The turtle eggs usually hatched at night and the tiny turtles had to find their own way back to the sea. They used the moonlight reflected in the sea as their guidance. On a clear night with a large moon, they usually didn't have any problems, but on the night of a new moon, or on a stormy night with clouds covering the sky, they might make a mistake and be led astray by some other light.

"That is why we ask tourists and guests not to put the lights on at night on their porches, and use thick black-out blinds in their rooms to prevent light pollution of the beach."

Moley liked this expression 'light pollution' and was promising himself to make sure that their condo didn't put the little turtles' lives at risk.

The only problem was – he still didn't know what turtles looked like. Ashley had been so busy yesterday with his swimming and shell hunting that he hadn't looked anything up about the turtles on his Dad's iPad, and so Moley didn't have the chance to sneak a peek over his shoulder.

The Turtle Watchers continued, pointing out a sign stuck in the sand on the edge of the beach:

"See how we ask people to remove their sun beds from the beach every night? This is also because of the turtles. If there are any objects left on the beach, grown-up turtles might get entangled in them and the young turtles might never manage to go around them and reach the sea."

'Hmm….' thought Moley, 'these turtles sound more helpless than even very young ducklings. Sounds like my nest-protecting and baby-animal-sitting skills might come useful here!'

Their guided tour continued and it was only now Moley realised just how many turtle nests were marked on the beach. Dozens, or even hundreds – as far as the eye could see in both directions.

"When we turtle-watch at night,' said Renee, 'we wear a special lamp on our heads. It has a red light in it. It's safer than the white light, because the young turtles cannot see it and it doesn't lead them astray."

"But another danger for baby turtles, of course, is predators," added Bob.

'Not predators again!' thought Moley in desperation. 'I had enough trouble with them at home, I didn't know they were in Florida as well!'

He listened closely and learnt that the most dangerous predators for young turtles were various sea birds – seagulls, herons, pelicans.

Because of that it was better if the turtles hatched at night, when the birds are asleep, not in the evening nor in the morning.

As the sun went higher and the beach got hotter, the turtle watch team shook hands with Ashley and Dad and agreed to keep them posted if anything interesting should happen. Then they parted ways and the Richardses went back to their condo.

That day Ashley looked thoughtful as if he had a plan. He went into his room, pulled a large flat round thing from his suitcase and said to Moley with a wink:

"You know what this is? It's a tent! A pop-up tent! It can pop up in a second and I am planning to put it to good use!"

Moley, for the life of him, couldn't understand what Ashley meant. But soon the mystery was revealed.

Ashley carried the flat thing outdoors, took it out of the zipped bag, twisted it lightly and – pop – as if by magic, a real tent stood on the ground in front of him. Bright red, with a yellow floor, triangular sides and a front entrance with a black zip.

"Wow!" exclaimed Ashley – he looked a bit taken aback himself, but, without a moment's hesitation, he unzipped the entrance and climbed inside, Moley in his hand.

"This will be our lookout post," he said to Moley. "When we do our own turtle-watch."

As they left the beach that evening, Ashley removed and folded down the tent, but left it outside on the terrace right by the sliding door.

Chapter Seven

A Crocodile and an Alligator

That night, after everyone had gone to bed, Ashley wrote a note for his Mum and Dad. "I am letting them know where we are going," he said to Moley, and left it on the coffee table in the lounge.

Then, with Moley in his right hand, he tiptoed across the room to the terrace door. He slid it open quietly, slipped outside, closed the door behind them and picked up the tent with his left hand.

The night was pitch black, even for Moley who could usually see in the dark pretty well. He found it hard to imagine how Ashley was managing to see anything at all.

Moley felt Ashley's hand squeezing him a little tighter and deduced that Ashley was somewhat nervous. Luckily, just then the moon came out of the clouds and lit up the narrow path across the grassy dunes. Ashley started down the path, balancing with his arms a little, as if walking on a narrow plank of wood.

They were only a few steps from the beach, but the walk seemed much longer than during the daytime.

When they reached the sand, Ashley did his magic twist and the tent popped up. Ashley unzipped the entrance, climbed into the tent and zipped it up again.

"You know, Moley," he said in a whisper. "I think they have snakes and crocodiles in Florida. Or do they call them alligators? I am not sure."

Moley didn't like the sound of that, didn't like it at all.

He'd seen crocodiles and alligators in Ashley's books and been – what is the word to use when you are scared but don't want to admit it? – Moley thought a little and settled on the word – 'impressed'.

Yes, he'd been *impressed* out of his mind with their wide snouts filled with long teeth that looked very sharp.

To be honest, at this point in time he didn't care much about which long word to use to describe these terrifyingly *impressive* animals – crocodiles or alligators – their teeth were long enough for either name!

Moley glanced around the tent. It didn't feel anywhere near as robust as it had seemed at first – definitely not robust enough to withstand a crocodile attack.

'You know what we'll do?' whispered Ashley. 'We'll keep the zip closed until morning, just in case.'

'But how will we watch the turtles then?' thought Moley, but didn't say anything because Ashley looked too scared, and suddenly discovering that his toy mole could speak might have been too much for him.

Ashley zipped up the entrance and checked that there were no gaps left in the corners, then he sat in the middle of the tent, hugging Moley tightly to his chest, his heart beating rapidly against Moley's little body.

Inside the tent was dark and silent.

Gradually Moley—for he was a mole who was used to seeing in the dark—started to see a little and hear a lot. He saw Ashley's big eyes with wide pupils looking down at him, he saw the walls of the tent. He heard the rhythmic sound of the waves, as if some giant was breathing softly in the night.

Suddenly, there came the sounds of sand crunching under something big and heavy. The sounds were getting louder, approaching their tent.

It was a crocodile or an alligator, for sure!

Ashley squeezed Moley and stopped breathing. They waited, frozen on the spot, hoping against hope that both the crocodile and the alligator would pass their tent without noticing it.

But the sounds of crunching sand drew nearer and nearer.

Ashley closed his eyes. Moley followed suit.

The time froze.

Suddenly:

"Ashley, are you there?"

It didn't sound like a crocodile at all! It sounded like Mum!

Then another voice followed: "Are you okay, Ash?"

And it wasn't an alligator – it was Dad!

At that moment Moley realised that there were no better sounds in the world than the voices of people you love.

Ashley drew in a huge breath, after holding it for so long, and shouted at the top of his lungs: "Yes, I'm here, we're here, me and Moley! We're alright!"

He unzipped the entrance and the worried faces of Mr and Mrs Richards appeared in the gap.

"I thought you knew better than this, Ash," said Mr Richards. "Going on the beach in the middle of the night, with only Moley for company! Not sensible at all, son!"

"I know," said Ashley, then added quickly, "but I left you a note. And I wasn't going to meet any strangers, so I thought it would be okay. I just wanted to protect the turtles," he added in a small voice, seeing that his father's face was still serious.

"There are better ways to do it, Ashley," said Mrs Richards. "Let's go into the house and we can talk about it."

Ashley, with Moley in his hand, climbed out of the tent, and Mr Richards folded it again in one movement before they all walked to the house.

It wasn't scary at all this time, Mummy went first, then Ashley with Moley, and Daddy with the tent – at the rear, making sure that his family was safe.

To Moley's surprise, Mr and Mrs Richards did not insist on Ashley going to bed straightaway. Instead, Mr Richards made everyone some tea, and they sat on soft chairs around the coffee table and talked.

It was a very good idea to talk a little before going to bed, because Moley was still buzzing with the recent excitement and knew he wouldn't be able to sleep anyway. He was sure that Ashley felt the same way.

Mr Richards, sipping his tea, began:

"As you know, turtles have been laying eggs on these beaches for centuries. In the past they always had dangers to cope with, but they adapted to them well, as the Turtle Watch told you. It all worked relatively well, until people came to these beaches."

"Typical," exclaimed Ashley, who had heard many stories of people endangering animals and felt very little sympathy towards the human race at such moments, albeit being its member himself.

"The humans started developing these beaches," Mr Richards continued, "building houses and hotels, bringing beach furniture and creating jetties. There were fewer and fewer places for turtles to nest."

"Yes, I remember," interrupted Ashley. "With the discovery of electricity, people's homes along the beach became very brightly lit and young turtles started getting confused – moving towards the houses after they hatched instead of the beach."

"Exactly," said Mrs Richards. "You see, we have a notice on the wall here that says to switch off our lights in the house or draw these blackout curtains across the window."

'To prevent light pollution,' remembered Moley, the expression he liked so well.

"And that is why we need to move all the furniture off the beach, as well, so that nothing stands in the way of a mother-turtle when she comes to lay her eggs, or when the young turtles go back to the sea."

"So, my tent could actually make it worse for the turtles," said Ashley, thoughtfully.

"Indeed," said Mr Richards.

"You see, Ashley," said Mrs Richards. 'Rather than staying on the beach the whole night, you'll do more good by checking it in the evening, to make sure that all the furniture is stacked away and all the lights are switched off."

They carried on making plans about helping turtles, and Moley noticed that his fright and the excitement of the last hour were subsiding. He felt calmer and it looked like Ashley did too. He even yawned a couple of times so that when Mummy suggested calling it a day (which meant going to bed) Ashley didn't say a word against it.

Chapter Eight

Twick and a Squabbling Squadron

The Richards family and Moley spent the next morning on the beach. Ashley, after making sure that he was far enough from any marked turtle nests, built a large sandcastle with massive thick walls, four round towers in the corners, and one square tower in the middle. The castle was surrounded by a wide moat, which filled up with sea water through the canal that Ashley dug.

This work took Ashley all morning, but, when the castle was finished, he put Moley on top of the highest middle tower, saying – "You'll be the guardian of this castle, Moley. I'm going for lunch, but will be back soon."

He ran away, leaving Moley quite alone, but Moley didn't mind, for in the bright Florida sun it seemed like there was not a worry in the world.

He sat there, watching funny little birds with long legs, who ran up and down the sea line, following the waves, quickly catching whatever food each wave would bring.

One of them came right to the wall of Moley's castle and Moley, although not sure whether the bird would understand him, called out: "Hello there."

The bird did a double-take, its mouth opened wide, and replied in a high-pitched voice:

"Gee! This thing can talk!"

Moley didn't like to be called a 'thing' and wondered whether to feel affronted by such an unceremonious address, but decided against it, for he really, *really* wanted to meet some locals.

"I am a toy mole, but yes, I can talk," he replied politely and rather formally.

"I am from the South of England, my name is Moley, and… (he very much wanted to add a line from Owlie's favourite television programme 'Pride and Prejudice': '…and I have five thousand a year', but he held his tongue in time and just added)…I am very pleased to meet you."

"Gotcha!" said the bird. "I've never met a toy mole before! Cool! I'm Twick and I'm from… this beach."

"Capital!" said Moley, wondering inwardly at the sudden old-fashioned formality of his own address. "You must know a lot about the local culture and customs. Pray tell me, are there any crocodiles on this beach?"

"Nope," answered Twick simply, and then continued with a quick rattle: "Crocs don't like the beach. Gators, same. They like swamps and long grasses. They come to the beach once in a blue moon, not often. In winter they like to plunge in a heated pool. To warm up. Get it?"

Plunge in the pool!

Honestly!

Moley now understood why the swimming pool on the side of their complex was surrounded by metal railing. To prevent crocodiles and alligators from taking a plunge in it! Who would have guessed!

'And what about turtles? Do you know about turtles?' he asked.

'Not much,' said Twick honestly. 'They're too big to eat. And not dangerous enough to be afraid of. So, I don't care."

At this point Moley noticed something large and noisy moving towards them along the sea front.

It looked like a huge screaming monster – with many heads, beaks and wings, moving, flapping and screeching at the same time.

"What is that?" exclaimed Moley, alarmed.

"Oh, no! Not again!" sighed Twick in exasperation. "Pelicans. Better keep away from them. We call that a pelican heap."

"What on earth are they doing?"

"They fight for fish," explained Twick.

It was quite a spectacle!

Moley had never seen anything like it!

A heap made of a dozen large birds moving along the sea edge, as if gliding above the water. But not gliding gracefully and serenely. Oh, no! They were fighting over something, beating their wide wings, sticking their long bills into the depths of the sea, throwing fish into the air and catching them mid-flight.

It was a spectacle, alright!

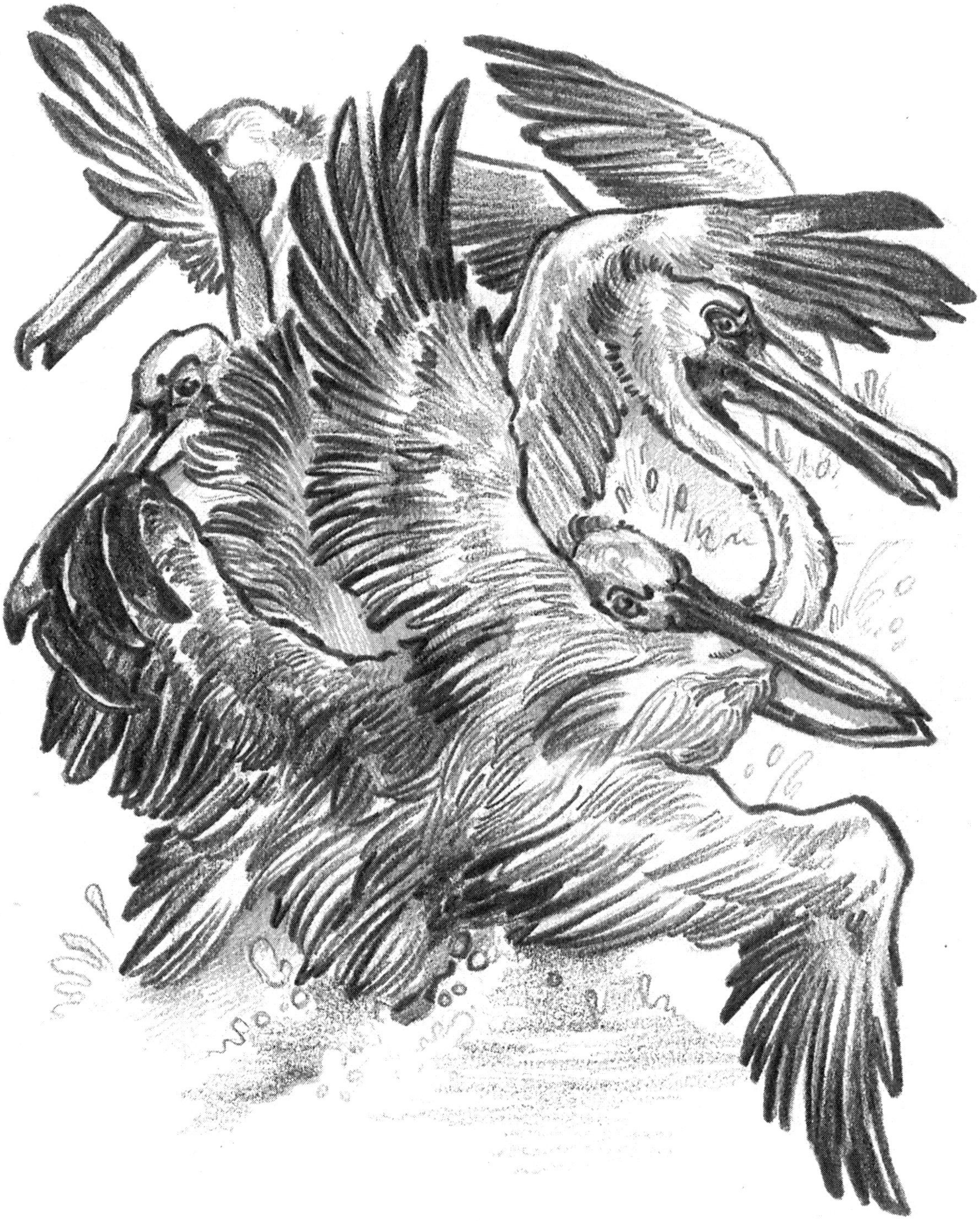

Suddenly, one of the pelicans broke away from the fighting heap and flew a few meters in the direction of Moley's castle, holding a large fish in his beak.

He landed near the moat and with a swift movement of his head flipped the fish into the air and caught it into his enormous bill. The fish disappeared whole.

'Wow!' said Moley. 'That's amazing!'

'Thanks!' The pelican turned his head to Moley. 'Holy Moley! What have we got here?!'

To tell the truth, Moley was lost for words.

Really, how he was supposed to answer, if a total stranger, on the one hand, knew his name and, furthermore, called him Holy, and, on the other hand, didn't seem to know what he was?

"I'm Moley," he replied at last.

The pelican tensed up. "Are you mocking me?"

"No, no." Moley rushed to disabuse him, for the pelican's bill **_impressed_** him very much indeed. "I am not teasing you, not at all! My name is REALLY Moley. But I am not sure that I am holy."

Moley suspected that he wasn't holy at all, but didn't want to give up entirely on this lovely idea. He liked the sound of "Holy Moley" quite a lot.

"If you're Moley, you must be Holy," replied the Pelican. "I've never heard of any other Moleys. Only Holy Moleys."

Moley felt he was on a shaky ground with this one and decided to change to topic: "But you are a Pelican, aren't you?"

'You bet I am!' replied the large bird. 'Have you seen such a bill on any other bird?'

"No, indeed,' said Moley. 'That is the most distinguished beak I've ever beheld."

('What's wrong with me?' he reproached himself. 'Why am I speaking like Owlie all of a sudden?')

"Dis-what? Did you call my bill dysfunctional?!" exclaimed the pelican aggressively, starting towards Moley again. "And did you call it a beak?!"

Moley felt that if he didn't remedy the situation quickly, the bird's beak, or bill, would be not only the most distinguished, but also the very final thing he'd ever behold!

"No, no, no, no, no, no, no," hurried Moley again. "I called it dis-ting-uished. It means special, unique."

"Are you saying I'm odd?" The pelican's tone was still tense.

"Not at all," replied Moley, racking his brains for another word. "I am saying your bill is very handsome and impressive. (It was impressive, alright.) It's fantastic. Yes, it is the most fantastic bill I've ever beh-- been in the presence of!"

"Okay then,", said the Pelican, somewhat reluctantly. "You better watch out, not many creatures can insult me and live to tell the tale."

"I can see why," muttered Moley under his breath but quickly added, aloud:

"And what is your name, may I ask?"

67

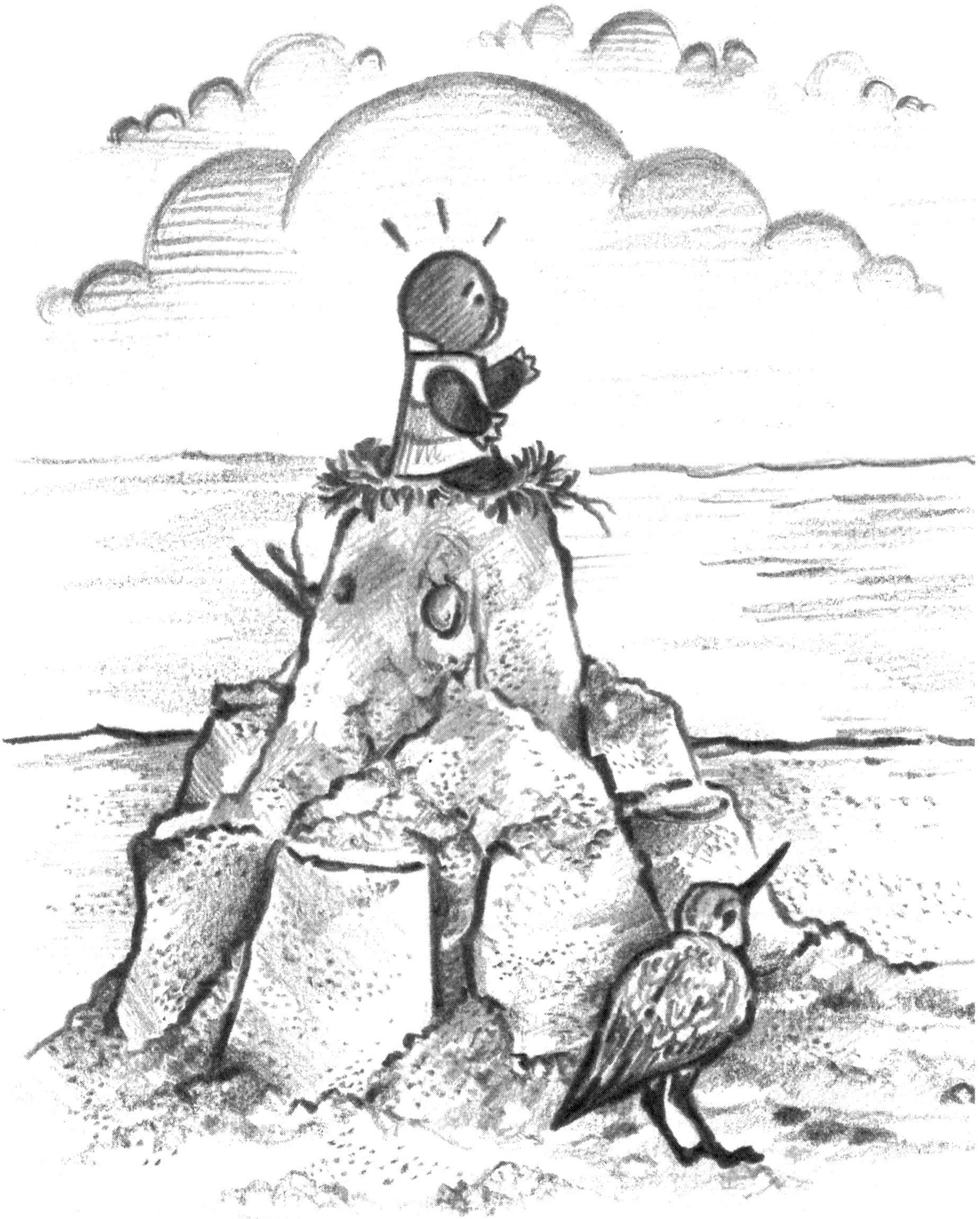

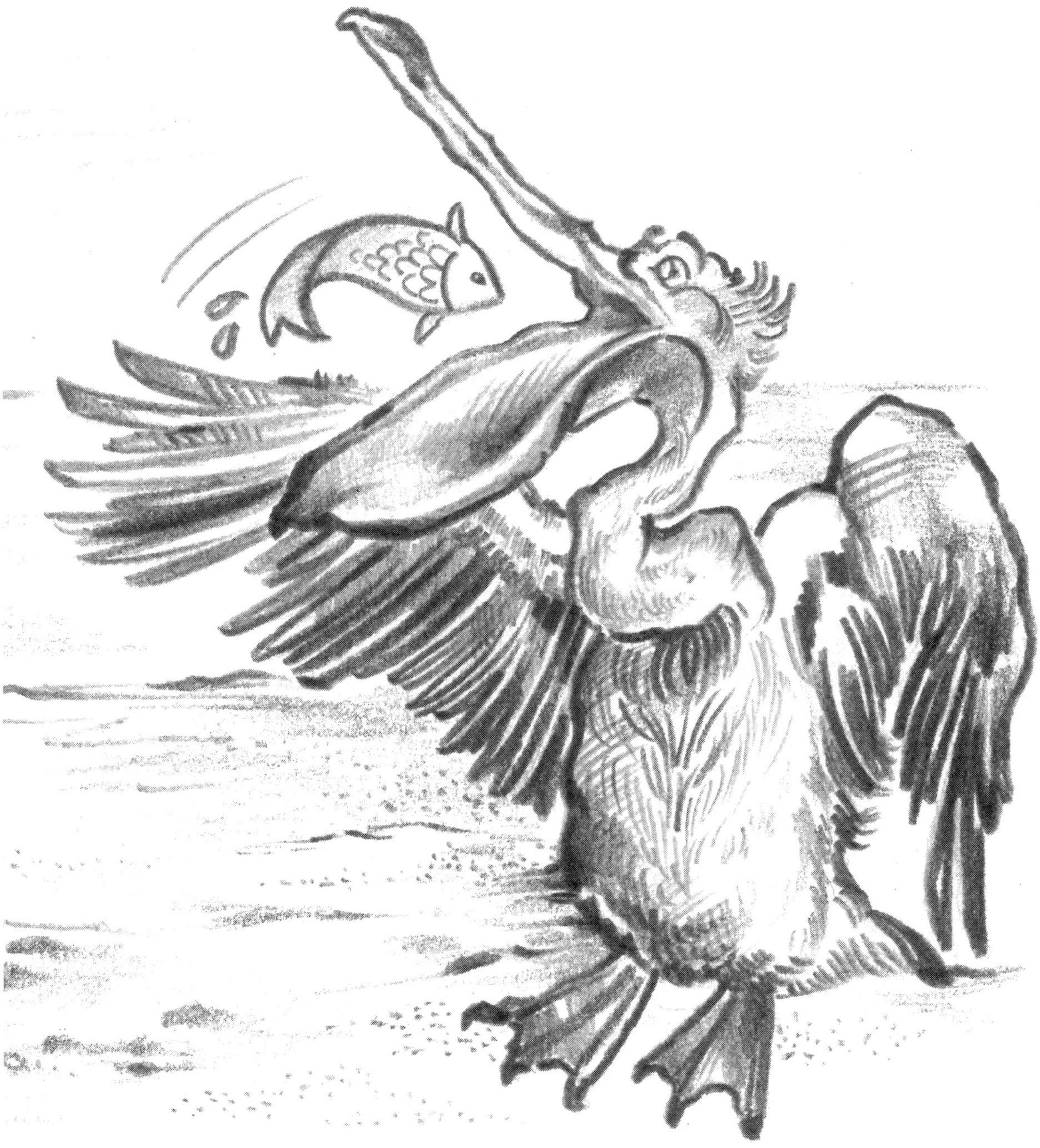

"You may," replied the Pelican, grandly. "Doesn't mean I'll answer," he added with a loud chuckle, giving Moley what he probably considered a friendly push with his bill. The push knocked Moley off his tower and he landed in the moat on his back – in the most undignified way.

"Holy Moley, what's up?" called the Pelican.

"Nothing is up," said Moley, grumpily, "I am rather down than up."

"Didn't expect you to fall like that, Holy Moley. I thought you were more robust."

'Typical,' thought Moley, 'now it's my fault that I'm not robust enough!'

The Pelican stretched his neck around the castle and with a word 'Gotcha!' pulled Moley out of the moat and put him back on top of the tallest tower.

Moley's bottom and back were wet and covered in sand and it didn't make him very happy.

"Well, Mr Pelican," he said, rather shortly. "Do you want to let me know your name or not?"

"My name is Dale. Lauderdale," replied the Pelican, unabashed. "Because I'm from Fort Lauderdale, see?"

"Lord Dale?" repeated Moley. "Are you really a Lord?"

"Why not? If you're a Holy Moley, I can be a Lord," replied the Pelican cheerfully. "Call me Lord Dale."

Then he thought a little and added: "Actually, can you call me Lieutenant Lord Dale? That would be great."

"Why Lieutenant?" asked Moley.

"It's my rank in the squadron," said Dale.

"The squadron?" repeated Moley. It was a new word for him, and he liked it.

"It's the formation we fly in," explained Dale in a tone that implied that Moley was rather stupid.

"Anyway, I gotta go and join the fight for the fish again. Or they'll think I'm chicken. See ya!"

With these words he pushed off with his large feet, spread his enormous wings and, knocking Moley over again with the air that rushed from under him, flew in the direction of the pelicans squabbling in the distance.

'What a character!' thought Moley, struggling to get out of the moat again. He was covered in a slush of water and sand from head to toe and wasn't completely sure he liked his new acquaintance.

Chapter Nine

Moley's Days and Nights

From now on the Richards family's routine was pretty much established.

They all went to the beach in the morning, when the sun wasn't too scorching. Mum and Dad pulled three sun beds down to the seafront and erected a large parasol over them. Ashley, however, didn't spend much time on the sun bed – he preferred to pop up his tent, which he used as a refuge from the sun in between his swims in the sea and his walks along the water edge in search of exotic shells.

There were quite a lot of those on a Florida beach, but because Ashley refused to take his bucket on these walks – "it wasn't cool enough for his age" – he kept his bucket in the tent, together with his lunch box and Moley. So, he constantly had to go back and forth between the water's edge and his tent with the handfuls of shells. In the tent he put them in the bucket, but he collected so many that he'd filled it up in a day or two. Then he took it inside the condo to empty into his suitcase and started again.

In the afternoon the Richardses usually went out in the car, exploring the nearby towns and parks, sometimes taking Moley with them, sometimes leaving him in the tent on his own. To make sure that the tent didn't fly away Ashley took two long lines that went from the sides of the tent and attached them to the pegs he made from broken-off branches lying on the beach, brought there by the sea.

He pushed the pegs deep into the sand and looked at his handiwork in a satisfied sort of way.

During these long afternoons, Moley sat at the entrance to the tent and chatted to many birds that were searching for food in the surf. Twick was there every day and so were his many brothers, sisters and distant cousins. They all looked the same to Moley and he had real problems distinguishing one from another, but they figured this out quickly and very helpfully started introducing themselves whenever they came to chat.

Like this:

"Oye, Moley, Twick here."

Or

"Oye, Moley, Twit here."

Or

"Oye, Moley, Flick here."

Their names were always short and when they talked to each other very quickly, all Moley could hear was: "Twit, twit, twit."

Sometimes they brought to Moley particularly pretty shells, when they spotted them in the water, and Moley managed to sneak them into Ashley's bucket before his return.

Dale came regularly too. He announced his arrival with a loud "Holey Moley!" and landed by the tent, sending a shower of sand into the air. He didn't stay long, because he was very preoccupied with keeping his rank in the squadron and it meant he had to always be in the thick of it, but he liked talking to Moley and learning new things about a distant land called England.

In the evenings, Mum, Dad and Ashley came back to the beach for another swim in the sea and then made sure that all their beach furniture was taken away.

They often had to tidy away other people's chairs and sun beds, because many people left theirs on the sand, not bothering to store them for the night. Ashley fumed every time he saw such behaviour and wanted to go and tell those people off, but Mr and Mrs Richards didn't approve of his urge to confront other holidaymakers and insisted that it was better to clear things away themselves rather than to seek an open conflict with their neighbours.

"We're all on holiday, Ash," said Dad. "Having a row never improves anyone's rest."

In the evenings, Ashley was the one who checked that all the blinds were down and not a single chink of light was escaping onto the beach.

Sometimes Ashley went on the beach patrols with his Dad, or his Mum, late at night. For these beach walks he wore a head lamp that he'd bought at the local museum. It was exactly like the lamp that the

Turtle Watch used. The light could be white, if needed, but Ashley set it to red – the light that would not confuse the turtles, for they couldn't see it, as the Turtle Watch had explained. Ashley, of course, took Moley with him on these walks and usually left him outside afterwards, propping him against a large cushion in a big rocking chair that stood in a middle of their terrace.

Ashley didn't mind leaving Moley there, for, by now, he knew that it was very safe on their island. Many people left all their beach things on the terrace overnight, not worrying about losing them, so Ashley started doing the same. Outside with Moley he often left his folded tent, propped against the wall of the building, his bucket with the sea shells, and his head lamp, thrown across the railing of the terrace.

At first Moley was worried to stay alone at night, but after the first night, he realized that it was not scary at all and happily stayed on the terrace afterwards.

Some mornings when Ashley woke up early, he and Moley went to see Bob, Renee, Monica and Ron, to hear the news and to chat with them about new nests on the beach. The Turtle Watch had marked a few nests as hatched and showed Ashley and Moley a small hole through which the little turtles had come out. They also told them that some little turtles didn't manage to exit the nest, because the sand from the flippers of other turtles buried them deeper and they couldn't dig themselves out.

That was very sad and upset Moley a great deal.

'Hmmm!" he thought. "That won't do! Why are all babies so helpless?

Another thing that bothered him was the fact that he still hadn't seen a single turtle. He imagined they looked like moles, slightly bigger, perhaps, with flippers for legs.

Well, because they were digging into the sand for their nests – this made sense to him. He imagined a turtle as an American mole, and really wanted to meet one.

Because he knew that turtles came out at night, and there were no reports of crocodiles or alligators on the beach, Moley took his chances, and despite his initial reluctance, started climbing down from his chair and wandering around the beach at night. Very close to the condo, to start with, then farther and farther away. The darkness wasn't much of a problem for him, as you remember, and he soon learnt all the nooks and crannies along the beach. Of course, he always put on his high visibility jacket, when he went on the beach at night. Better safe than sorry, was one of his mottos.

Chapter Ten

A Creature in Distress

One night, Moley went onto the beach very late, or, some people might call it rather early, and wasn't sure he would see anything interesting at all, until he heard some movement in the tall dry grass right at the top of the beach behind the sun beds piled up for safety. Whatever it was, it sounded like something rather large.

'A crocodile! was Moley's first thought and he froze on the spot, impressed. The rustling continued and Moley's curiosity got the better of him. He moved a little closer.

As he moved closer, he started hearing long low moans and sounds of something heavy hitting the pile of sunbeds.

Hmm…said Moley to himself. It sounds like an animal in distress, and even if it is a crocodile, it might be in trouble and I should try to help.

Very cautiously he edged himself around the sun beds until he saw a huge animal of a kind he'd never seen before.

It had a hard dome-like structure on its back and a flat bald head on a wrinkly neck. Also four legs ending in flippers which it was using to push forward with all its might, hitting its head on the pile of sun beds, moaning softly in a low, hoarse voice: 'Oh no, oh no, oh no…'

'Stop!' exclaimed Moley, who felt very sorry for the creature. 'Just stop and listen! Please!'

He thought that the creature couldn't hear him in its distress, but the head-banging stopped for a second and Moley hurried forward.

"Look at me. I'm here, right here on your right. I'm here to help."

The creature moved its bald head on the long neck right and left and right again, until one of its eyes caught Moley's dark shape and fixed on him.

"That's right," said Moley soothingly, and remembering Owlie's unsuccessful attempts at counselling a few weeks back, decided not to ask the creature how it was feeling. It was clearly distressed. Moley didn't need any verbal confirmation of that.

"I am Moley and I am here to help," he said again in a firm voice. "Do you want to tell me your name?"

The creature looked at him with one wide-open eye, clearly in disbelief and confusion.

Eventually it made a long loud exhale and the eye blinked.

"What are you?" it asked slowly.

"I am Moley. I am a mole, a toy mole," said Moley and added, just to have something to say, "I'm here on a holiday from England."

The creature stared at him silently, probably still in shock.

"What are *you*?" asked Moley.

"I'm a turtle," said the creature.

Despite the gravity of the situation, Moley did a silent mental fist pump: 'Yes! Finally, a turtle!'

"Do you have a name?"

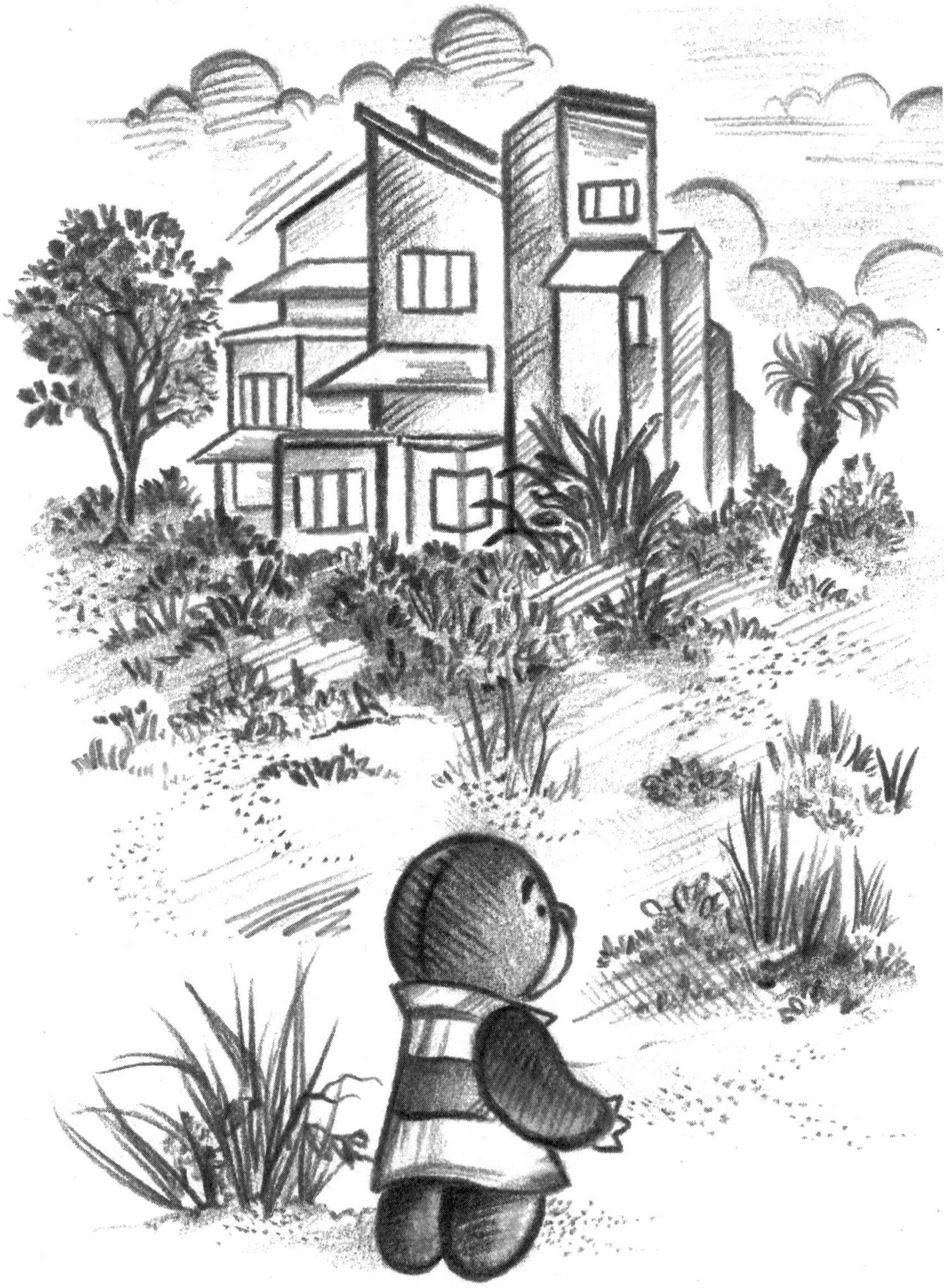

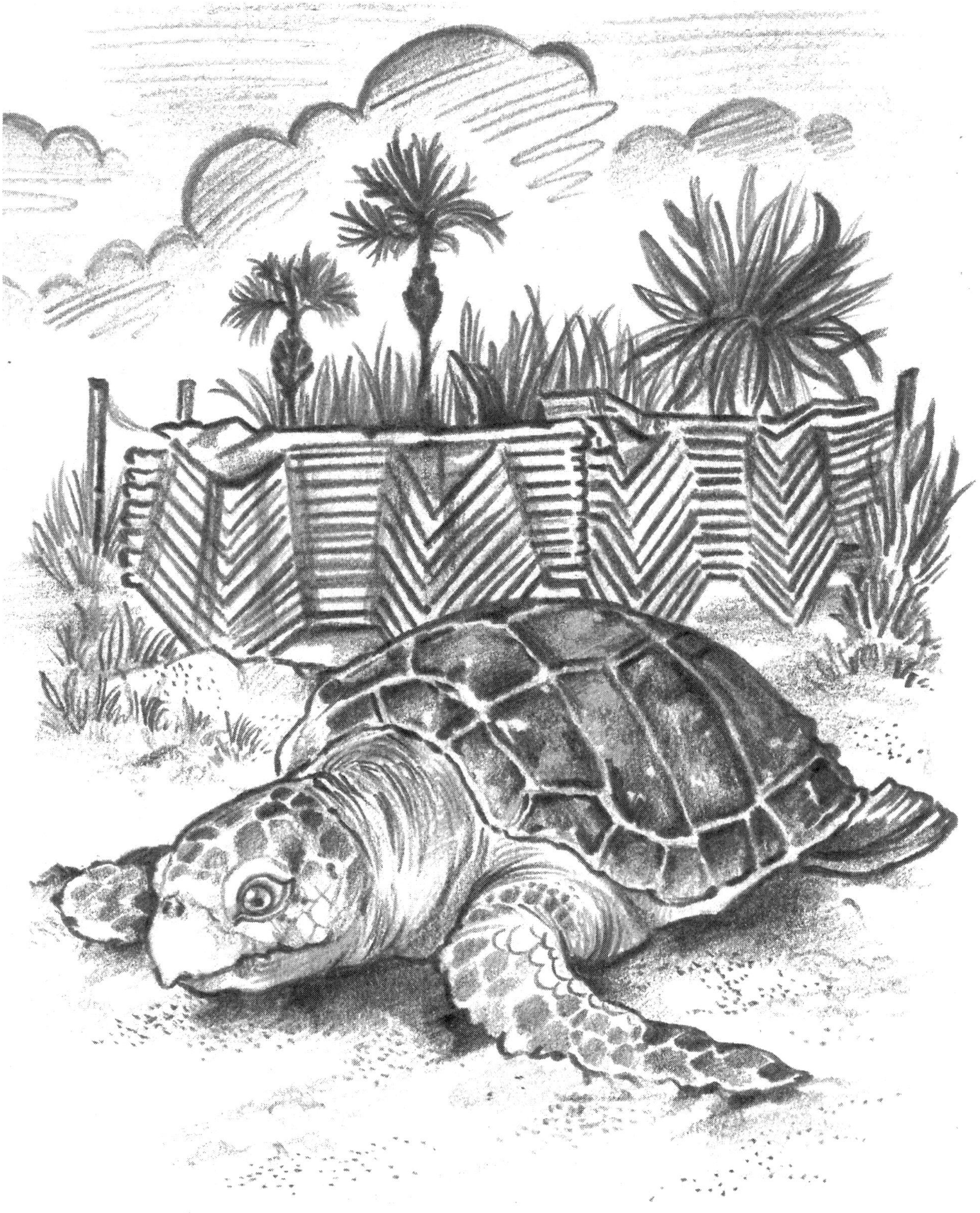

"Yes."

"Do you want to give it to me?"

"No, I want to keep it for myself."

'Hmmm…' thought Moley. 'She understands things literally, I'll try again.'

"What is your name?"

"Shelly."

"It's a pretty name," said Moley. "And suits you very well."

"So, you don't want me to give it to you anymore?" asked Shelly.

"No, you can keep it," said Moley, deciding on the spot that now wasn't the right time to go into a lengthy explanation of the actual meaning of his words. "Tell me what you are doing here, Shelly."

"I laid my eggs and I want to get back to the sea, but I can't get past this wall."

'Just as I thought,' said Moley to himself.

And then to Shelly: "This is not a wall."

"Yes, it is," said Shelly.

She likes to argue, thought Moley and said aloud: "Well, it is a very short wall and I can show you the way around it. Follow me."

He started to walk along the side of the sun beds, aiming to turn around the corner. But Shelly stayed put.

"What now?" asked Moley, getting annoyed, ever so slightly.

"We only walk in a straight line," said Shelly. "We don't go sideways. It's our way."

'Oh, bother,' thought Moley, returning to the turtle.

"Ok, let's do it this way – there are many ways of walking in a straight line. As long as you turn in the right direction before you start walking, you'll never walk sideways. Look!" – and he started to push Shelly, gently turning her whole body in the right direction.

'Gently' didn't do it, though, and he had to push really hard to make her move. Once she was facing the right way, Moley commanded: "And now – go straight", and they started their journey.

At every corner this procedure had to be repeated until eventually they were on the final straight towards the sea.

Shelly felt better once she could see the water.

She turned to Moley and said: "Thank you, little toy mole on a holiday from England, you saved me. Would you also look after my nest? It's my first one. I've hidden it in the long grass, so that no one steps on it. It's just behind the wall I was stuck at…"

"I shall," replied Moley. "Will you come and see me again?"

"I shall," said Shelly and, surprisingly quickly, moved towards the sea, leaving a perfect turtle track behind.

Moley was delighted with the night's work.

'Clearly, not only babies need help,' he said to himself. 'Grown-ups also might feel helpless when they are in unfamiliar circumstances. Lucky I was there!'

Moley stood by the sea for a while, hoping to spot Shelly in the waves, but she was gone, and he decided to go and check on her nest before everyone was up.

He found it quite easily because he knew where it was, but he was sure that the Turtle Watch people would not look so far from the water's edge, in the tall grass, behind the pile of sun beds.

By now Moley knew that they used turtle tracks to show them where the nest was and Shelly's track back down to the beach was quite visible, but at the top of the beach it was almost non-existent, because the sand there was very dry and it had filled in the track almost completely.

What could Moley do?

He really wanted the Turtle Watch people to see Shelly's nest and mark it so that it had been counted and protected. This was really important.

And then the idea came to him. Ashley's bucket full of shells was still standing on the porch and Moley decided to make use of it.

He started picking shells up one by one and laying them in a line from the end of Shelly's track all the way to Shelly's nest.

He had a few shells left to put them all the way around the nest.

By the time he'd finished he heard the voices of the Turtle watch approaching and all he could do was to collapse next to his handiwork and pretend that he'd been there since the last night.

He heard Monica's voice: "Oh, look, this is unusual."

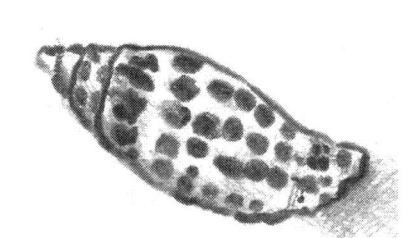

"Really unusual," agreed Renee.

Bob made a guess.

"I think Ashley was out last night and must have seen the turtle laying the eggs in the grass. Look, he marked the nest for us to find."

"Ah! You must be right!" said Ron. "And he dropped his toy mole!"

Ron picked Moley up and cleaned the sand from his back.

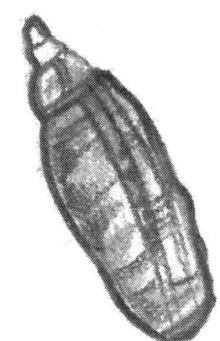

"That was very clever of Ashley," said Monica and all four of them started their usual routine of surrounding the nest with yellow sticks and orange tape and recording the date on one of the sticks.

When the job was finished Ron went to the Richards's porch and carefully placed Moley on the rocking chair.

"Ashley will be pleased to find him," said Monica and the Turtle Watch continued their walk along the beach,

looking for more

new nests.

Chapter Eleven

Endangered Species

From now on, Moley started checking Shelly's nest whenever he could. There was nothing much to see, really. It didn't change very much from day to day, but Moley had given a promise and therefore kept an eye on it, at least making sure that it remained undisturbed.

At night, Shelly came to talk to him now and again. She didn't go to check the nest, but rested on the beach, where the water met the sand, and asked Moley questions about his life. Moley told her about his home and his garden, his friends, and his flight on the plane. Shelly often shook her head in disbelief, but she didn't argue, like she had the night they'd met, for she wasn't as distressed as she'd been then. And when she wasn't distressed, she wasn't argumentative at all.

She also told Moley about her life in the sea.

"I am a green turtle and I was born on this very beach," she said.

"Oh, so you haven't travelled much?" asked Moley, feeling quite proud of his travelling achievements so far.

"No, not very much," agreed Shelly. "I've only been around the world a couple of times. I am a very young turtle."

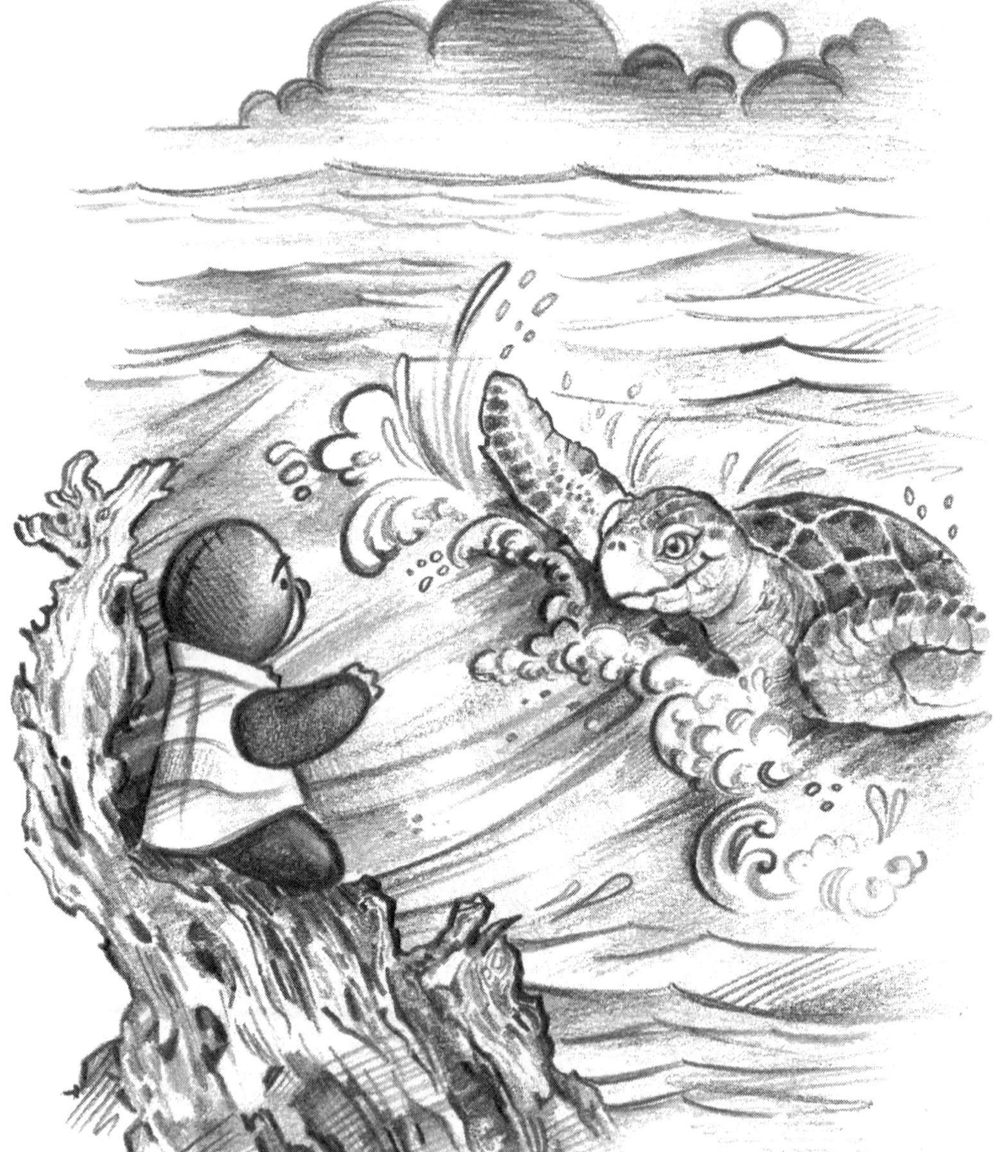

"A couple of times around the world!" exclaimed Moley aloud, and thought to himself: 'That puts my own travelling to shame!'

"Yes," continued Shelly. "I am a very young turtle. The youngest in my family. Only twenty-five. Because turtles live long. My grandma is 80, but that's nothing. Grandma has a friend, a Leatherback called Uncle Leonard, he is at least one hundred and fifty years old. Maybe more. He doesn't know for certain."

"Have you seen a lot of the world?" asked Moley.

"I've seen all the seas, but not much above the water. We try to avoid humans, whenever we can."

Moley was surprised: "Why so? Most humans I know are very nice – well, except, my previous owner, Lorna. But what is the chance of you meeting HER!"

"Humans are not regarded well by us, the Green Turtles. And I am sure it has nothing to do with your previous owner, Lorna."

Shelly told Moley about the times when hundreds and thousands of Green Turtles were hunted by men and sold at big markets all over the world, so much so, that now there were not many of them left.

Moley guessed: "So, you belong to an endangered species! I know what that means."

Moley was sorry for Shelly and her relatives, and felt even more responsible for her nest now. "I'll keep an even better eye on it," he assured Shelly.

"Thanks," said Shelly. "But don't change your eye on my account. Your eye is good enough. No need for a better eye."

Shelly, as usual, had taken things literally.

"Anyway," she continued, "after all our travels, we, the sea turtles, come back to the beach where we were born, to lay eggs and have our young. It's our way."

"Do your children find you in the water after they hatch?" asked Moley.

"No, it's not our way. They have to fend for themselves, just like I did," replied Shelly, somewhat irresponsibly, in Moley's opinion. However, remembering his experience with Alexis, the Mother Duck, when he'd been completely wrong about her nest, and she was right, he decided not to express his view to Shelly. Following his recent resolution 'Trust the Experts', he said to himself that she was the mother; she, surely, knew best.

There was one point in the story though that was not fitting in.

"How do you know your Grandma, then?" asked Moley.

Shelly made a strange crackling sound, and Moley guessed that she was laughing.

"I call all old turtles 'Grandma'. It doesn't mean we are related," she said. "It's our way."

'How odd,' thought Moley at first, but then it crossed his mind that he called Mrs Richards 'Mummy' and Mr Richards 'Daddy', even though he wasn't their son. 'All families are different,' he concluded in his head. And he was happy with that conclusion.

Chapter Twelve

Brad the Crab

One day Moley was sitting by the entrance of the tent having just finished his brief, as ever, chat with Dale, when he saw two eyes looking at him from behind a small sand dune.

That was the thing.

They were just eyes. No head. No other part of the body of the creature they belonged to. Well, there were two sticks these eyes were attached to, but that was it. Two eyes on two sticks.

Moley stared back. He found it difficult to decide which eye to focus on because they seemed strangely separate.

Suddenly the eyes disappeared and, in a moment, appeared again.

"Hello," said Moley, tentatively.

The eyes disappeared.

"Hello," Moley said a little louder.

The eyes popped up again.

"Can you hear me?" asked Moley, thinking that the eyes might not be able to hear. Because they were not ears. And if he tried to talk to the eyes, which were not ears, he would look a little bit stupid.

The eyes looked to both sides and then a voice come out of nowhere.

"He's gone?"

"Who?" asked Moley.

"Big Bill."

"You mean the pelican? Yes, he never stays long. He needs to protect his rank in the squadron."

"Right." The eyes looked both ways again. "You eat crab?"

"No, I don't eat anything," replied Moley earnestly.

"Right," the voice said again, and suddenly the eyes started moving sideways along the top of the dune. And soon, from between the two dunes out came a funny little creature with a flat back, ten legs (lucky there were only ten, the exact number Moley could count to!) and two eyes sticking up from its shiny body. His two front legs were bigger than the others and shaped like pincers and the creature lifted these up in greeting.

"Hey," he said.

"Hello," said Moley. "I'm Moley, and you?"

"Brad. Brad the Crab."

"It's got a nice ring to it," said Moley, trying to be polite.

"Ring? Where? What ring? A trap?" The crab's eyes were scanning in all directions.

"No, no, no. No ring and no trap," Moley reassured him. "All good."

"Big Bill your friend?"

"Yes. He is," said Moley, "He's a lieutenant in his squadron and he flies on the lefthand side of his leader."

"I don't like him. He eats crab," said Brad.

"I see," said Moley. "Well, he's not coming back soon, don't worry."

"If he comes, you tell me," said Brad. "I'll dig in." And he pointed downwards into the sand.

"Oh, so you can dig?" Moley was glad. "You know, I can dig too. Not as well as real moles do, but I can. You see, my paws are very wide."

"Want to dig together?" asked Brad. "We can dig up a turtle nest, and I can eat the eggs. You - don't eat. You're a cool dude. Cool dudes don't eat."

Moley was horrified and disgusted.

"You? You're a predator? You're so small and you're a prey for big birds, and yet you're thinking of eating someone else's eggs?! How dare you? Green turtles are endangered, did you know THAT?" Moley's voice was shaking with indignation.

"All crabs eat eggs," replied Brad, simply. "Grown turtles eat us. It's life, it's cool."

Moley didn't like the sound of that, but decided to be honest with Brad: "You see, I promised to look after the nest of my friend, Shelly.

It's her first nest, and I can't allow anything happen to it. If you or any of your relatives decide to attack it, I will have to fight you."

"You're bigger than me," said Brad. "I'm not gonna fight you. Let's make a deal."

"What deal?" asked Moley.

"You give me food better than eggs," said Brad.

"Like what?" asked Moley.

"Worms!"

"I don't have any."

"Shrimps."

"Nope."

"Fruit?"

"Yes!" Moley felt excited. There was always left-over fruit in Ashley's lunch box, because Ashley was too busy on the beach to eat.

"You bring me fruit. I like fruit. Then I help you by not eating the eggs," said Brad.

Moley thought about it. This danger to the nest was new to him, he'd known nothing about it until this conversation. How many other dangers didn't he know about? It would be really useful to have a local predator on his side, a small predator, he could negotiate with. It surely was worth a few pieces of fruit from Ashley's lunchbox that lay in the tent every day, practically untouched.

"Alright," said Moley. "It's a deal."

"Let's shake on it!" exclaimed Brad the Crab excitedly, and stretched one of his pincers towards Moley.

Moley gave him his paw, and Brad pinched it rather painfully.

After that he kept the pincer stretched out, and Moley realised that the deal had to be fulfilled straightaway.

He went into the tent and opened Ashley's lunchbox. There were several pieces of apple there, and a few grapes. Deciding not to spoil Brad on the first day by giving him too much, Moley picked one slice of apple and took it out of the tent. Brad grabbed the offered fruit and rushed away sideways, without a further word.

Moley only had to hope that the crab would keep his word and help him to protect the nest.

Chapter Thirteen

A Brazilian Free Tailed Bat

From that day Moley's afternoons were rather busy – checking on the nest, chatting with Twick and his many friends, having a brief word with Dale, and feeding Brad – it was as full on a day as one could imagine, but it soon became even busier.

For Brad decided to tell many other crabs about a strange creature from a foreign land who was giving away lovely treats in exchange for not digging up turtle nests.

On the second day there were two crabs waiting for Moley by the tent. On the third – three. On the next Moley counted to ten and gave up. They needed a lot of food, or they were going to destroy all the nests on the beach. "It's blackmail!" exclaimed Moley, but he couldn't think of any other way of keeping the nests safe. So, he carried on emptying Ashley's lunchbox of all the fruit every day.

The good thing was that Mrs Richards, when she noticed that all the fruit was being eaten every day, started putting in more, and not just fruit, but vegetables too. She was very pleased with Ashley's healthy eating, and Moley felt a little guilty. But he didn't have another option. He did what had to be done for Shelly's nest.

Of all the things Moley offered the crabs, Brad and his gang liked cucumber and grapes the most. On the days when Ashley didn't have these favourites in his lunchbox, the crabs sulked, digging themselves into the sand all around the tent, only leaving their eyes sticking out, looking at Moley reproachfully. When they did that, Moley took the opportunity to lecture them on the advantages of eating different fruit and veg, rather than fellow animals. He hoped that his words sunk in.

After such busy days Moley enjoyed his lonely night vigils on the terrace very much.

The air was cooler, filled with a mixture of the exotic smells that during the day were burnt out by the sun, it seemed. Moley could smell the salt from the sea, the sharp fishy odour of the seaweed, the sweet fragrance of night flowers and fresh scent of the lawns, watered nightly from the sprinklers hidden in the grass.

The nights seemed very quiet at first, the only sound being the sturdy, rhythmic breathing of the ocean, but the longer he sat on the terrace, the more sounds he could distinguish in the darkness.

He heard the distant calls of night birds, the rustling of the tall dry grass along the beach, a low buzzing of bush crickets, and high-pitched screeches of some unknown to him animals.

In all this multitude of sounds he didn't notice at first a quiet voice – yes, voice! – that was actually talking to him.

Looking around, he couldn't see the speaker at first. He was searching the terrace's floor and the sand around it. But the voice was coming from above.

"Look higher, I am here," it said.

Moley looked up and saw a big winged creature, hanging upside down from the roof of the terrace.

"Is it you talking?" Moley asked.

"Yes, it's me."

With one flap of its leathery wings the creature moved to the arm of Moley's chair, where it settled down, folding them neatly. It now looked like a furled-up black umbrella with a little pig face.

"Who are you?" asked Moley in astonishment.

"I am a bat," said the creature.

"A bat! I've heard of bats," exclaimed Moley, and bit his tongue, for many of the things he'd heard were not very complimentary.

"Out with it," said the bat. "I know all sorts is said about us."

Moley was abashed. It was as if his new acquaintance could read his mind.

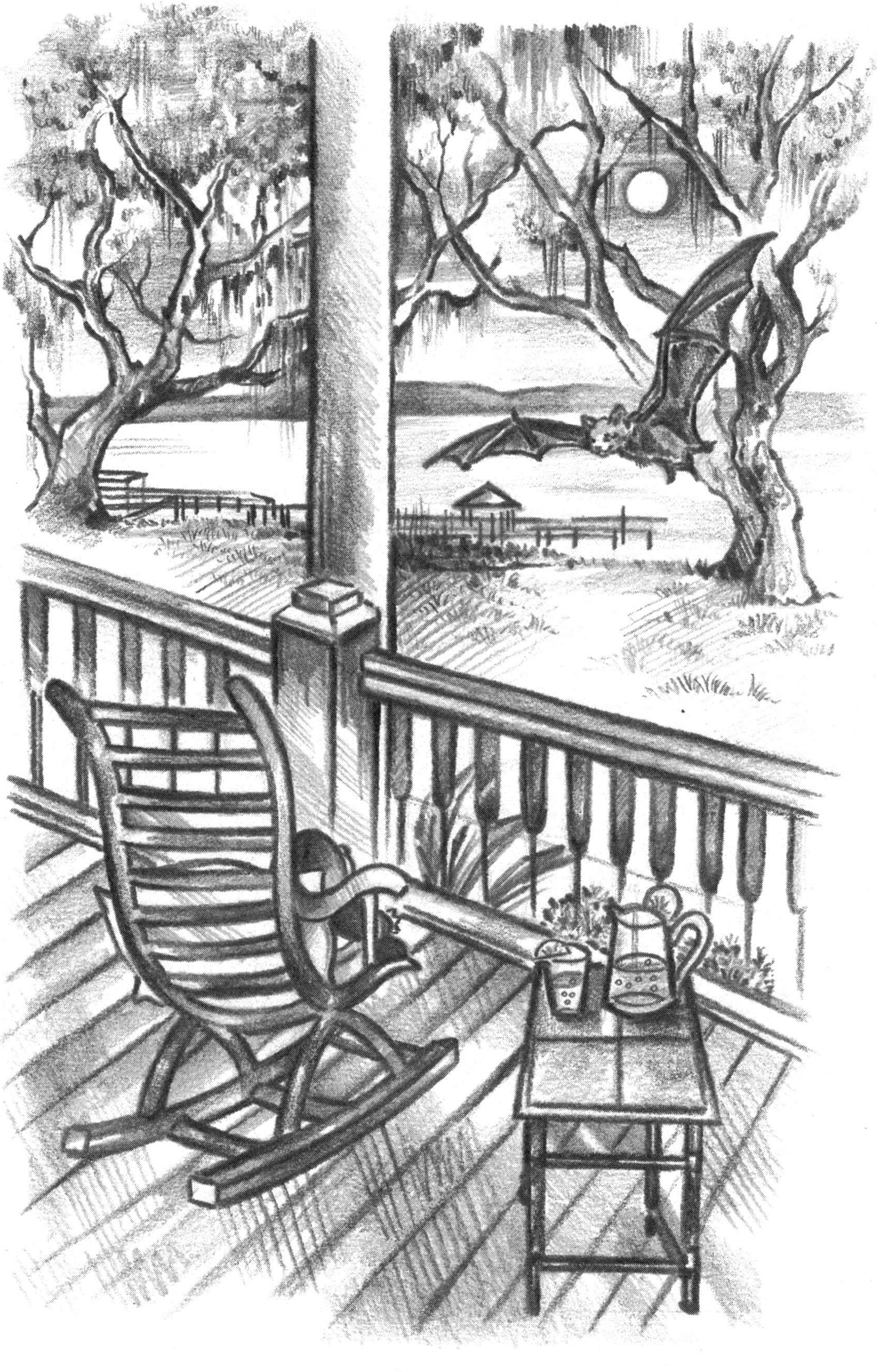

"Don't worry," he replied. "I don't believe everything I hear."

"Well, let me guess," sighed the creature. "You've heard that we are rodents, and vampires, and all of us have rabies. Correct? None of it is true. I am not a flying rat, I don't suck blood, and I don't have rabies."

"But," it continued, "I can fly for hundreds of miles each night, faster than a car, and I use ultrasound echolocation at night. These things are true."

Moley's heart was won over that instance!

"Ultrasound Echolocation!" He simply had to become friends with a creature who used such words!

"Very nice to meet you," he said with a bow. "I am Moley, and I am honoured that you've decided to talk to me."

"I am Bruna, a Brazilian Free Tailed Bat. And the pleasure is mine."

Moley was delighted to make another friend, especially one who could talk so eloquently and politely. He missed the long, meaningful conversations he had with his friends back home, for his new acquaintances, although very friendly, usually didn't say very much.

Bruna was well informed, reflective and very intelligent. She reminded Moley of Owlie a little. Owlie also was thoughtful and smart. Moley wondered whether the fact that Bruna and Owlie both were creatures of the night had something to do with them being clever and insightful. Perhaps, one has to become insightful, when there is not much light outside?

Moley was most interested in Bruna's Ultrasound Echolocation.

He had come across the word ultrasound before. Mr Richards, who was a surgeon, mentioned it sometimes as a way of seeing things inside the human body. But Moley believed you needed a special machine to do that. He asked Bruna to explain and she said:

"Humans might need machines for this, but we bats don't. We can send our ultrasound signals in every direction and receive back the information about all sort of things. This is called echo-location, you understand? Our signals go, hit an obstacle, and return to us as an echo. This way we know what is there, how far and how hard. It is a very useful thing in the dark."

Moley remembered his adventure with an X-Ray machine at the airport.

"Is it like the x-ray?" he asked.

"I don't know what the x-ray means," said Bruna honestly, "but, yes, our ultrasound goes like a ray and comes back to us with the information."

Moley was really pleased both with her honesty and the things he was learning. Clearly, there were many ways to see inside things – x-ray and ultrasound. If only he could make use of this unique ability of Bruna's.

And he had an idea!

"Can you send your signal into the ground?" he asked.

"Why not?" said Bruna.

"Can you send it through the turtle nest and check whether the eggs are OK?"

"I believe I can," said Bruna.

"Let's do it!" exclaimed Moley. He climbed down from his chair and led the way towards Shelly's nest. Bruna flew silently behind him in the dark.

When they reached the nest surrounded by the yellow sticks, Moley pointed it out to the bat: "Here."

She hovered over it, sending her signals, but Moley couldn't hear a sound. That was because they were ultra-sounds, above his, and humans', ability to hear,

After a while Bruna turned to Moley and reported: "The ultrasound scan is complete. There are 125 eggs in this nest. They are healthy and not yet ready to hatch."

Moley was delighted and proud.

And he was right to be proud!

Without knowing it, he'd organised the very first turtle antenatal clinic on Tortuga Kay, with its own ultrasound scan!

***

Now Moley's nights became just as busy as his days.

With long conversations with Shelly and Bruna and almost nightly ultrasound scans of the nest, he hardly had a free moment to spend time by himself and think his own thoughts.

But it was all worth it!

He was protecting endangered species – nothing could be more important in his opinion!

Chapter Fourteen

Operation 'Nest'

One night Moley sat on the terrace in his rocking chair quite alone. Because he hardly had any time to himself nowadays and nowanights, he was enjoying this rare solitude, and used the opportunity to think at least some of his own thoughts while looking at the dark sky.

There were many stars over the ocean, because it was the night of a new moon, so there was no moon in the sky at all, and the stars were not outshone by their much larger companion. All the windows of the condos in their development had gone dark, as everyone obeyed the regulations very strictly. 'No light pollution', said Moley to himself in a very satisfied way. The complete darkness made the observations of the stars particularly rewarding.

He was trying to count them, which was a challenge made harder by the fact that he, as you remember, could only count confidently up to ten. But Moley, who had never been deterred by something so trivial as the inability to count beyond ten, had devised his own, quite shrewd, system. He climbed down from his chair, pulled closer Ashley's bucket full of today's picking of seashells, and started counting the stars by putting aside a shell every time he reached ten. That gave him the idea of how many tens of stars he'd counted so far. He had six shells laid aside already and was progressing his count towards the seventh.

Moley, of course, didn't know multiplication, but can you help him? How many stars will he have counted by the time he's put aside seven shells?

Anyway, he had six shells laid aside already and progressed his count towards the seventh, when several things happened in very quick succession.

A door slammed above his head – and someone walked into the condo directly above the Richards'.

A bright light came on in the top-floor window – the newcomer had switched it on, not knowing yet, perhaps, that it was forbidden.

At the same time a pair of leathery wings flapped loudly and Bruna landed next to Moley.

"Bruna' exclaimed Moley. 'Where have you been?"

"I was scanning Shelly's nest." replied Bruna quickly. "I told you last night that the time was near. Now the time has come."

"Oh, no!" Moley didn't know what to do whereas Bruna seemed more composed.

"Let's go there," she said and flew ahead, Moley close in her wake.

They had come just in time. The first few little turtles were already out of the nest, with their brothers and sisters behind quickly digging themselves out of the sand hill made by their mother. And –

sure enough—in the darkness of the night they all took the immediate direction towards the brightly lit window on the top floor.

"Oh no, no, no, no," shouted Moley, panicking. "We need to stop them, we need to turn them towards the sea."

But how?

Trying to stop the increasing flow of young turtles was like trying to stop a stream of water with your bare hands.

What could Moley do?

The idea came to him suddenly.

The light!

The light was the key. They needed to block the light that led the turtles in the wrong direction and start a light that would lead them to the sea.

And he had that second light. The head-lamp that Ashley used at night had two settings, red that turtles couldn't see and bright white. The one they needed now.

But before going to the terrace to fetch the lamp he needed to stop the baby turtles from going towards the condos.

"Brad!" shouted Moley. "Brad, I need you!"

And to his amazement, two eyes on the sticks popped up out of the sand straightaway. And not just two – more and more pairs of eyes were appearing all around him, a whole field of eyes on the sticks, all looking at him penetratingly, waiting for his instructions.

"Brad, I appoint you as leader. Your task is to keep the turtles away from the buildings, and, particularly, the swimming pool. That water might kill baby turtles." Moley said decisively. "Do everything you can. I'll be back."

With these words Moley ran back towards the terrace, but noticed through the corner of his eye that Brad had raised both his claws in the air and started clicking them, making a noise very similar to the one humans make with their fingers. "Y'all, do what I do!" he cried. Other crabs copied him, spreading across the turtles' path, blocking it.

Moley ran up to the terrace, Bruna leading the way above him.

"You seem to have a plan?" she asked.

"I need a lamp!" shouted Moley, reaching the terrace. "That one, see?"

He pointed at the strap hanging on the railing out of his reach.

'Easy,' said the bat and flew straight under the lamp's strap.

She was beating her wings very quickly, and the strap slid off the rail in no time falling straight into Moley's outstretched paws.

"You are a star!" he shouted to Bruna.

"Sure, if you say so," she replied, and Moley could hear a smile in her voice. "Anything else I can help you with?"

'If only we could turn that light off somehow."

He pointed at the bright window on the floor above.

"Easy," said Bruna again and produced a very high-pitched sound, one of those Moley could hear at night sometimes, not knowing what they were.

All of a sudden, dozens, if not hundreds of bats were flying towards them from all directions.

Bruna beat her wings again and rose into the air, leading the way. All the bats followed her, going towards the lit window. A few moments later the window was invisible for the masses of beating wings, all clinging to the glass.

"That is amazing, Bruna! Very impressive!" shouted Moley, putting Ashley's head-lamp around his own chest and turning it on. He switched it from red to white and the bright beam cut through the darkness, clearly illuminating the path to the beach.

Moley hurried down the path towards Shelly's nest and saw there another impressive scene. Very impressive, indeed.

Dozens of tiny sea turtles were moving in all directions, facing away from the sea, trying to go toward the condos where a lit window had been recently visible. But facing them was a long line of crabs, their pincers in the air, making clicking sounds, not allowing the turtles to move any further inland.

"Brad," called Moley. "Brad, you are all brilliant!"

"Sure thing!" he heard from down the long line of crabs.

"Look at me!" called Moley to the tiny turtles. "Look at my light!"

They were already turning in his direction. One, two, ten, all of them were moving towards him and Moley knew that his plan was working. He walked tentatively backwards, towards the sea, the light shining from his chest.

The turtles followed, crabs at the rear, nudging the slow ones in the right direction.

Moley crossed the beach and stopped at the water's edge. He knew that it was time to switch off his light, but wasn't sure the young turtles would all find a way to the sea.

And, at that moment, he heard the voice.

"Come, come to Mummy."

108

Moley turned around and to his astonishment saw that Shelly was there, in the water, her big shell shining with the light reflecting from Moley's white lamp.

Moley stood fast so that the light shone directly onto Shelly's shell and the baby turtles ran into the sea to their mother, one by one.

Moley watched them disappearing into the waves, inwardly wishing them the best of luck. He knew that their life in the ocean would be full of dangerous challenges, and worried about them, of course, for he was a worrier. But, on the other hand, he also knew that they were over the biggest hurdle – getting back to the ocean safely and he felt proud that he and his friends had played their part in this safe deliverance. Furthermore, he knew that this lot had a very good chance in the ocean, for their Mother had decided to stay with them, help them and guide them. There was nothing better to wish for.

At this point his thoughts were interrupted by Brad, who arrived at Moley's side, having thanked the other crabs before they left the scene.

"Moley," said Brad. "The others. Remember?"

Brad's economical way of talking was so familiar to Moley by now that he understood him at once.

He remembered the story he'd heard from the Turtle Watch about the smallest turtles not always making it out of the nest.

It was the time to become a real mole! And dig!

Moley was quite nervous about it. At the end of the day, he was a toy, his paws were soft and his claws – even softer, for they were made of pink felt. But he wasn't the kind of mole to be easily defeated. He believed that what one was missing in physical abilities, one could compensate for in determination and perseverance.

Head-lamp still on across his chest, Moley turned around and hurried after Brad, who led the way.

Shelly's nest looked almost untouched. Only a small hole on the side indicated that the little turtles had left it.

Bruna appeared from nowhere. "My sisters are going to deal with that window without me," she said. "I'll help you."

She sent her ultrasound signal deep into the sand and said: "Several of them are still there."

"I'll burrow," said Brad. "You follow."

With amazing swiftness, the crab started digging with his legs on one side, disappearing from view almost at once. Moley followed, as he was instructed.

The sand was dry and light and digging into it wasn't difficult at all, but the problem was that it covered the hole almost as soon as it was made. Moley didn't give up, but soon he realised that on his own he wouldn't have been very successful at all. Luckily, Brad had more experience of burrowing in Florida sand and soon he was coming out, pushing a little turtle in front of him.

"One," he said. And disappeared again. Moley took the turtle in his paws and ran to the sea.

"Go, go, go!" he urged the baby turtle, placing it in the surf, but Shelly was still there, and the little turtle found its way into the water, following its Mother's calls.

Moley ran back to find another turtle already brought up by Brad.

"One," said Brad and passed the baby turtle to Moley. Moley took the second turtle and ran to the sea again.

They worked all night. Moley's legs were wet and covered in sand, his fur dirty too, but he kept running up and down the beach until the sky turned pale blue and the first hint of pink became visible on the horizon.

At last, Bruna scanned the nest and said: "That's it. All done."

Brad came out of the burrow with a long happy sigh.

"How many did we save?" asked Moley.

Brad looked up at him with his round black eyes.

"One," he replied.

For he only could count to one, poor thing.

"Hmm," said Moley, "I think it was about ten."

And he blushed inwardly and promised himself to learn to count beyond ten.

"Twenty five," said Bruna. "You saved twenty five."

She gave them a wave and flew away to sleep, for that is what she usually did during the day.

Moley and Brad walked slowly to the water's edge and in the first light of dawn they saw Shelly, surrounded by all her children, waving goodbye to them.

"Thank you, Moley, thank you, Brad!" she shouted, before turning and disappearing into the depths of the beautiful briny sea.

"And thank you, Bruna," added Moley, remembering his friend and her large family.

Chapter Fifteen

Moley Can't Catch a Break

Ashley found Moley in the morning, covered in sand from head to toe, lying on the terrace surrounded by shells, head lamp dropped nearby.

'What happened here?!' exclaimed Ashley. 'Were you attacked?'

He picked Moley up and cleaned him gently, then he put up their tent and placed Moley inside, thinking his little friend could do with some sleep after the rough night he'd evidently had.

"We are going to a theme park today and will not be back until the evening, then I'll remove the tent and take you home. Okay?" said Ashley.

Moley didn't mind. In fact, he was grateful for that. He was, indeed, very tired and could do with some rest and relaxation.

By now the story about the night adventure had spread through the beach. It wasn't surprising at all, for all the night moths had watched it unfold and all the little crabs had actually participated in it, so the word got out. Naturally.

Mid-morning Moley was woken by a tap on his shoulder and when he opened his eyes, he saw a large bill hanging over him. Dale's head was inside the tent, his body still outside.

"Holy Moley!" came the usual greeting.

"Ah, Lord Dale," said Moley. "Hello."

"Only have a sec," said Dale. "I'm on duty today."

"You're always on duty," muttered Moley.

"I heard about your adventures last night, dude. Twick told me," continued Dale in a hushed whisper. "And I want to say – well done, bro. I wish I could do something as heroic as that."

Moley felt flattered, but his sense of fairness didn't allow him to accept this high praise without protesting.

"There was nothing heroic in what I did," he said. "Anyone would have done the same."

"Don't know about anyone," said Dale, shaking his head. "Most of my pals would've eaten the turtles rather than save them."

"Good job I'm not a pelican then," said Moley, before adding: "You wouldn't have eaten them, would you, Dale?"

"I don't know what I would've done," said the pelican honestly. "I can't plan that far ahead. I can only deal with the situation in front of my bill."

"I better be off," he added, looking over his shoulder. "My major will be displeased. See ya!"

And he was gone in a blink.

"Fair enough," said Moley and closed his eyes, sleep taking him over instantly.

He was woken again by the sound of thunder – a storm had come out of nowhere as often happened in Florida.

Moley poked his head out of the tent's flap and recoiled in fear.

The sky was dark, with low clouds rushing across it at top speed. Blindingly white lightning slashed the clouds in several places at once. These were followed by thunder so deafening it sounded like the sky was crashing down to earth.

After the big storm Moley had lived through back home in England, just a few weeks previously, he thought he'd seen it all. But this was a storm of mammoth proportions – fierce and relentless. Moley had never seen anything like it.

"I'll be ok," said Moley to himself. "I'll just sit here in the corner of the tent and wait for the storm to be over."

He pressed his little furry body into the corner when the tent gave a shudder. Then another one. Then the entrance flaps flew open, and a strong gasp of wind filled the tent, lifting it off the ground. The strings holding the tent, attached to the pegs, were stretched to the limit and soon the pegs were pulled from the sand.

The tent was flying! Gaining height with every second, speeding away from the beach, spinning in the wind.

Moley curled up in his corner, holding tight to the walls of the tent, terrified and slightly sick. The tent's loops and spins made him light-headed and all he could hope for was not to be thrown out in the next somersault. He lost track of time, was he flying for a few minutes or a few hours? He couldn't say.

Only when the thunder had died out and his flight became a little smoother, he opened his eyes and tentatively moved towards the entrance to look out.

The tent was flying over an island. In a way, it was a good piece of news. If the wind had taken him into the sea, the chances to find land would have been very slim indeed. Moley didn't know what island it was, but hoped it wasn't too far from the one he'd set off from.

The wind was dying out, and the tent was gradually losing height. That could have been a positive development, if Moley hadn't spotted a wide ribbon of a road underneath, packed with cars, speeding along one after another. What if his tent landed right on the windscreen of one of them? It might cause a terrible accident.

Moley had to prevent the forthcoming disaster. He needed to find a way to steer the tent away from the road.

He looked out of the entrance flaps and noticed the strings with the pegs still attached to them. The other end of each string was tied in a knot inside the tent and Moley had an idea. He grabbed one knot, then rolled across the floor and grabbed another. Pulling each in turn, he figured out how he could steer the tent in one direction or the other.

After some getting used to it, he managed to turn his flying house away from the road, inch by inch, and slowly direct it towards the wide deserted beach on the right.

Steering the tent firmly, he made sure that it didn't fly towards the sea, but stayed above the beach, gradually descending, until it touched down gently and came to a stop on the soft white sand.

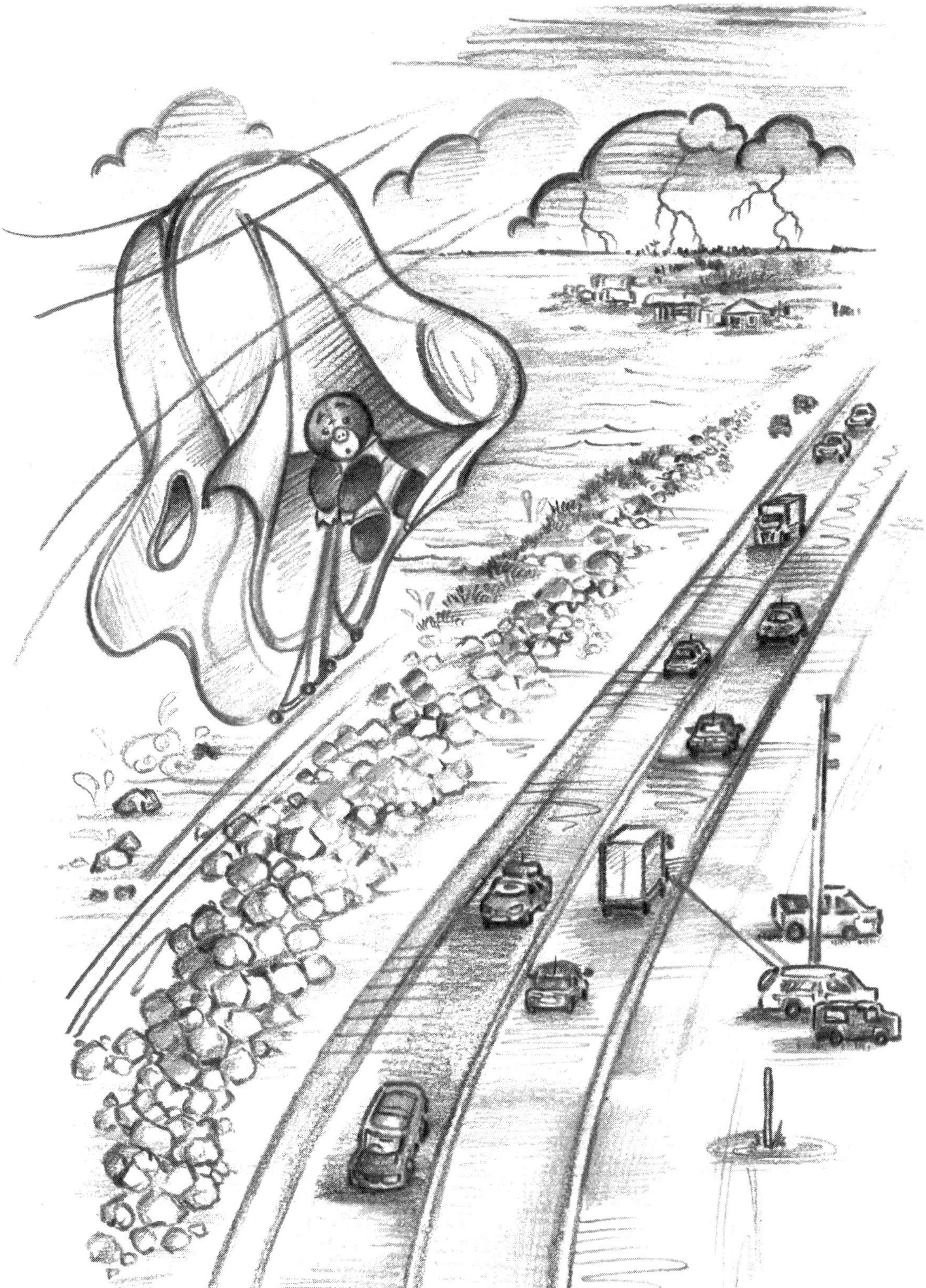

The storm was over.

Moley was safe.

Quite safe and quite alone.

Chapter Sixteen

The Mysterious Flying Dot

Moley crawled out of his tent, his paws still shaking after the excitement of the flight. The beach was stretching in both directions as far as the eye could see, with the beautiful turquoise sea glittering in front of him all the way to the horizon.

Dry grass whispered softly behind him; there wasn't a creature in sight.

Moley had no idea where he was and how to get back to the people he loved. He usually didn't give in easily, but this time he felt he was beaten. He had no clue where to start.

He sat on the sand in front of his tent and hung his head.

He was lost.

Completely lost.

Even if someone finds him on this beach one day, they will be complete strangers. A new family. They might take him home, or might throw him in the bin.

He will never see Ashley again.

He will never see his old friends – Owlie and Boris, Ludwig and Alexis...

He will never even see his new friends – Bruna, and Brad, and Lord Dale...

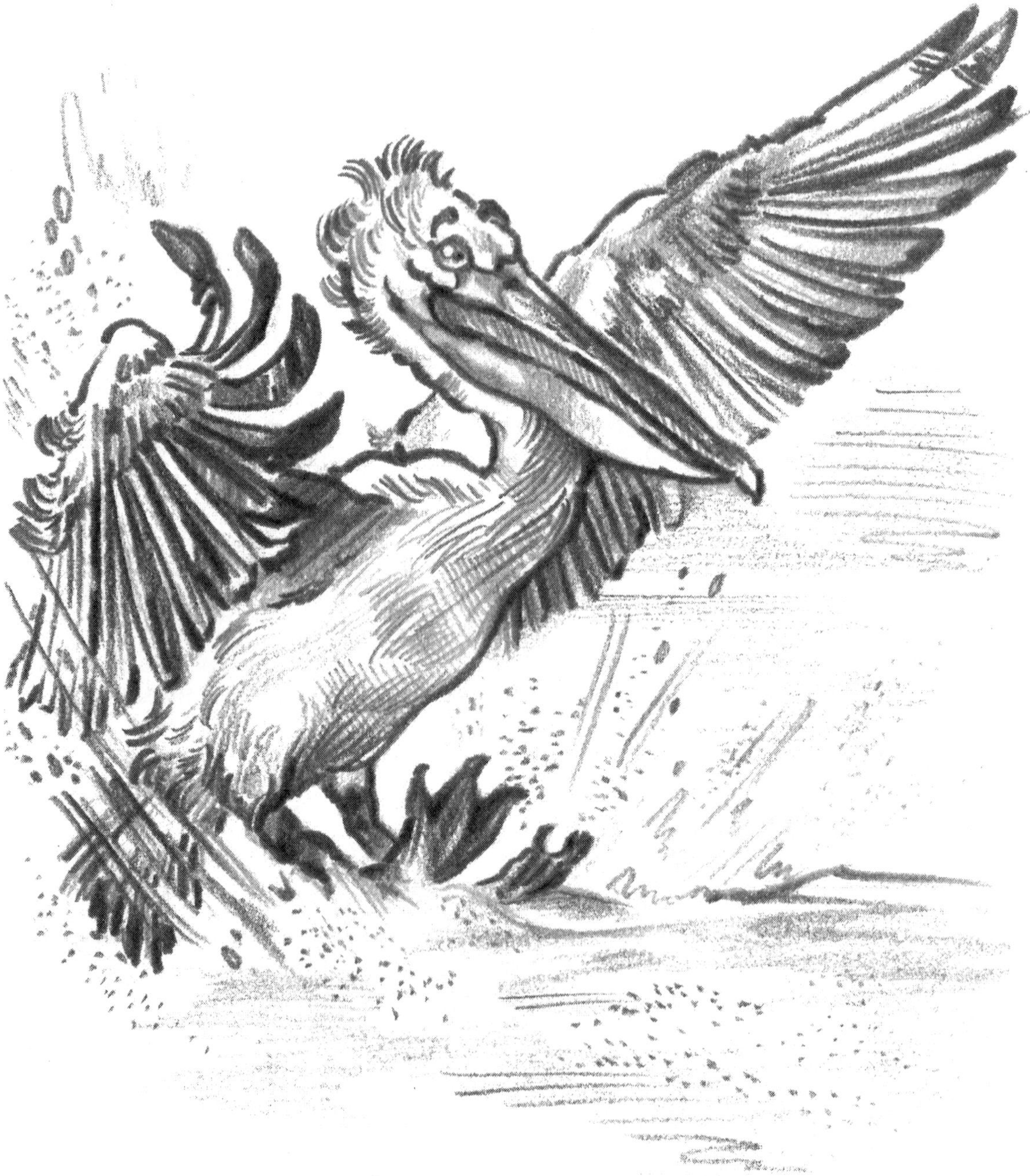

With a big sigh Moley raised his head and looked at the horizon, fighting back the tears.

But wait...

What was there – in the sky? A dot... a flying dot.

With his eyes full of tears, Moley couldn't quite figure out what the dot was, but he was sure it was getting bigger, and bigger...

Bigger and bigger...

Until it became VERY big with wings spread wide and the bill opened in an exhilarated smile.

"Holy Moley! I am coming! I've got you, dude!" shouted Dale exuberantly.

(For it was Dale, of course! There was no one else in the world with such a voice and such a smile!)

"Dale!" Moley couldn't believe his eyes. "What are you doing here? How did you find me?"

Dale landed next to the tent with a loud bang of his wings, leaving two long brake tracks in the sand.

"I followed you!" he shouted. "It wasn't easy but I followed you all the way!"

"Followed me?!" Moley was astonished. "But how did you know that I was in trouble?"

"Twick," replied Dale shortly. "Twick saw you taking into the air and came to tell me. The little guy knew that his wings would not be strong enough to fight the wind. And he was right! Even MY wings struggled in the storm. And they are much bigger!"

Moley knew that at this point he had to pay a compliment to Dale's wings. But it was easy this time, for he was truly, truly grateful and impressed.

"Your wings are amazing, Dale! I don't think any other bird could have coped with that storm!"

Dale looked pleased.

"But wait!" a thought crossed Moley's mind. "If you are here, it means... it means... you left your squadron and position!"

"Yep," replied Dale shortly. "I thought of it, but only for a sec. There wasn't much time to think, dude. You were flying away real fast – if I thought too long, I'd have no chance to catch up. You are my friend, Holy Moley, I had to do it. There was no other way."

Moley couldn't believe his ears.

Dale, who cherished his position in the squadron so much, had left his place for Moley – it was truly remarkable.

"Thank you, Dale! You saved me," said Moley.

"Hey, that's what friends are for," said Dale, smiling widely.

"It was heroic, Dale," said Moley. "You are a hero!"

"What?!" Dale looked astonished. "I always wanted to be a hero, but I became a hero when I least thought of it! Really?"

"It is often the case, you find greatness when you don't look for it," said Moley, and liked how wise this sounded. "But what will you say to your commander?"

"I'll think about it when I see him," replied Dale.

"I'll come with you when you do that," said Moley.

"Nice!" replied Dale.

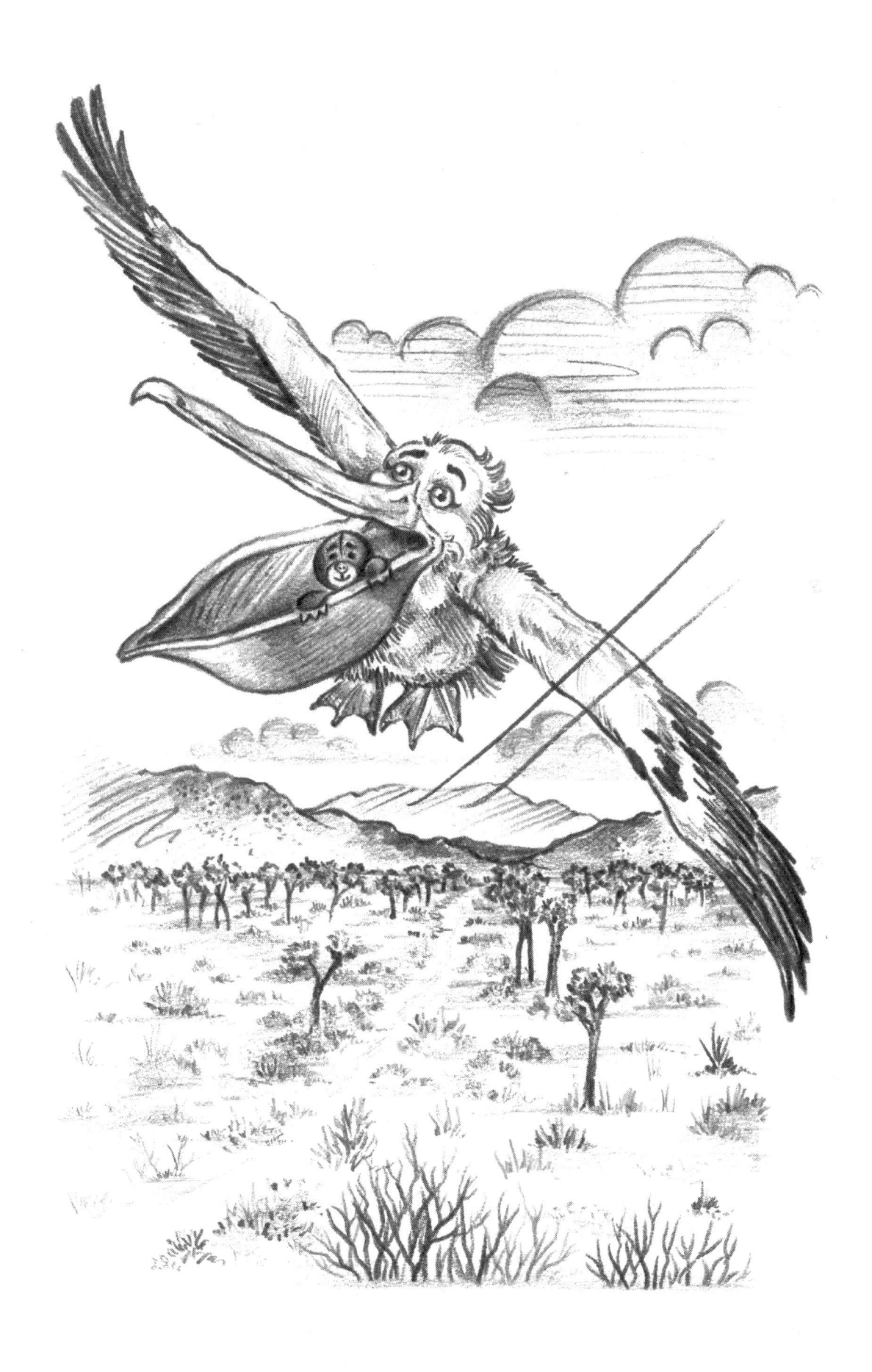

"Now we need to get back," he continued, getting very serious. "There is no way I can carry the tent. It'll have to stay here. I'll only take you."

Moley felt a little ping of sadness at the thought of leaving his wonderful flying home behind, but the sadness was short-lived. Compared to the desperate situation he'd been in just a few minutes ago, leaving the tent seemed a small price to pay for being rescued. Nothing was more important than getting back to those he loved.

"Okay, Dale," said Moley, "you are in charge. If you say it should stay, it will stay. Just help me to fill it with sand and pebbles, so that it doesn't fly again and cause an accident."

With these words Moley started throwing sand inside the tent, but Dale said shortly: "Move over."

He filled his bill with sand and emptied it inside the tent, then again and again. After only three bill-loads the floor of the tent was covered with a thick layer of sand that pressed it firmly down to earth.

"That'll do," said Dale.

"Fabulous," said Moley.

"Ready to go?"

"Totally," said Moley.

"Climb into my bill and hold onto the side. Don't stand on my tongue, I might retch you out, and don't let me shut it, I might swallow you."

'Charming,' thought Moley sarcastically. But kept it to himself. After all, beggars can't be choosers – and he didn't have any other way to get back. He climbed into Dale's bill, clinging to its side for dear life, quite scared to let go or to step onto Dale's tongue by accident.

Dale didn't say anything – for Moley was in his mouth now. He made two big steps, pushed off the ground and rose into the air.

Epilogue

When the Richards family returned home to England from Florida they were tanned, full of happy memories and, as Daddy put it, salted through like gherkins.

Moley couldn't wait to see his friends and to tell them everything about his adventures on the other side of the ocean.

They listened with great attention, each of them finding a different part of his story particularly interesting.

The dogs, Rosie and Rusty, really liked the bit about the crabs and how Moley had trained them to eat fruit and not to eat little turtles. "That's right!" said Rusty. "You can train any animal if you put your mind to it."

The dinosaurs, Bronti and Dina, liked the part about the turtles. "Turtles lived in the dinosaurs' time," said Dina, "and survived until now, unlike us. I am glad you helped them not to be extinct."

Boris, the bear, approved of Dale's bravery, not only of him flying through the storm, but also risking the disapproval of his senior officer. "When a life is in danger, you need to use your own head," said Boris. "No time to wait for the command."

Moley was pleased to hear that because, in fact, it was exactly what Dale's squadron commander had said to Dale upon his return. Dale was quite nervous facing him, for he'd left his squadron to follow Moley's tent without permission. He came to see his leader with his head hung low. But ... his commander said: "You did well, Lieutenant Dale. You used your own judgment and initiative in a life-or-death situation and saved a friend. You deserve to be promoted to the next rank and to form your own squadron."

So, by the time Moley and the Richards left Florida, Captain Dale was already flying at the head of his own small, but chivalrous squadron.

Owlie paid attention to all aspects of the story, and was especially impressed by the bat and her ultrasound echolocation.

"We have bats in England too," she said. "I see them flying across the night sky, but I had no idea they are equipped with such special powers. I must try and talk to one sometime. They sound fascinating!"

When Moley finished his story, Owlie looked at him with her large protuberant eyes and said:

"The thing you should be most proud of, Moley is how you've managed to bring all these different creatures together, to work for the common good. Just think of it, some of them would never even see each other, like crabs and bats, some would eat each other – like birds and turtles—but you brought them together and they achieved something quite remarkable. Well done!"

Moley felt very pleased and his nose got a little pinker, which meant he was blushing, and to hide his delight he turned to his friends and said:

"Enough about me, what about you all? How are the ducklings? How is Moley-Two?"

To his surprise everyone started laughing.

"Moley-Two?" they cried. "More like Molly-One!"

"What do you mean?" asked Moley, perplexed.

"Your duckling turned out to be a girl," giggled Rosie.

"But don't worry," added kind Bronti, "we still call her after you – only not Moley, but Molly."

Moley, having finally understood what they were talking about, joined the laughter.

***

One Saturday, two weeks after their return from America, Ashley, his parents and Moley sat downstairs around the large dinner table, and played a board game Ashley had invented. It was called "Save the Turtle", and required four players, each playing with a counter marked with a name: Monica, Ron, Renee and Bob. Moley was playing for Monica today, but as he couldn't move his counter in front of his humans, Mum, Dad and Ashley moved it for him in turn.

Suddenly a small red van with a Royal Mail logo on its side drove through the gate and a few seconds later a postman called at the door.

Mr Richards went to answer it and returned to the room with a neat little parcel in his hands. Moley noticed a picture of an animal that looked a bit like a black and white bear on the label, and the letters WWF.

The parcel was addressed to Ashley and he opened it keenly with a pair of scissors he fetched from the kitchen. Inside the parcel there was a letter, a colourful magazine and a soft toy. Not just a soft toy! A turtle! A little green turtle!

Moley couldn't believe his eyes!

Ashley unfolded the letter. "It's from the Turtle Watch," he cried.

The letter read:

Dear Ashley,

Thank you for all your help with protecting the turtles over the summer.

We hope you had fun.

To help you to remember this holiday and everything you've learnt about sea turtles, we've adopted a turtle on your behalf through the World Wildlife Fund – WWF. You will be receiving information from them about sea turtles and how to help them all year round.

And the toy is for you to keep.

Come again soon.

Renee, Monica, Ron and Bob

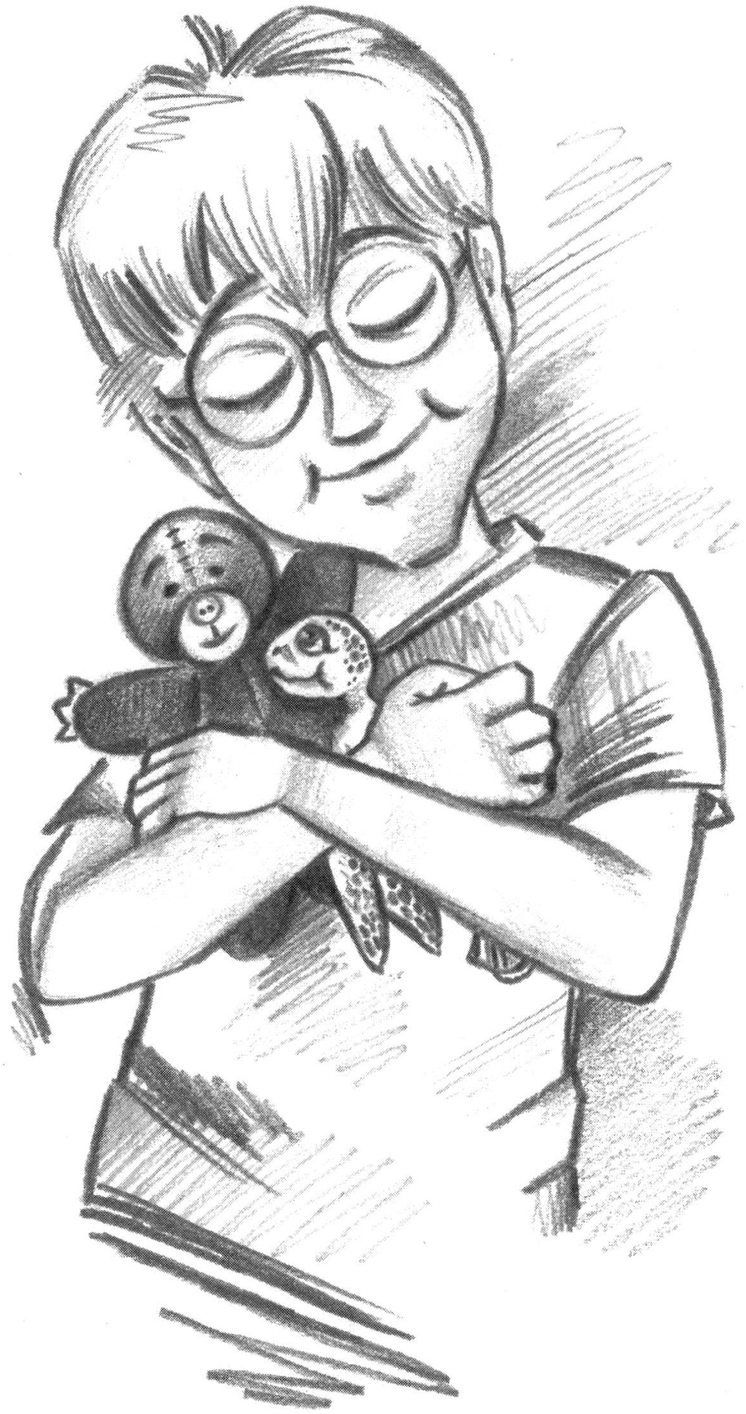

Ashley pressed his new friend to his chest, but because he was a very fair person, he pressed Moley to his chest with his other hand too. Moley's head was right next to the turtle's.

"Hello," whispered Moley.

"Howdy," she whispered back.

"What will you call your turtle?" asked Mummy.

"She's got a very nice shell," said Ashley. "I'll call her Shelly."

The End

More about Moley

Do you know that Moley is a real toy?

He lives in Sussex, UK, with Julia, the author of this book, her family and his friends and goes on many adventures that don't always end up in a book.

Do you want to follow his day-to-day adventures?

You can!

Look at the next page and find how...

Follow Moley and his Friends on Facebook:

@Moley and Friends

facebook.com/AMoleLikeNoOther/

Check what Moley's up to on Instagram:

@moley_and_friends

instagram.com/moley_and_friends/

Subscribe to Moley's YouTube Channel and join him on his journeys:

@moleyandfriends

Search for Moley & Friends

Readers' Reviews
of A Mole Like No Other

I loved reading about Moley and his adventures! I'm so glad he was taken out of his box and to a new family. I hope to have my own Moley one day, so we can go on adventures too.

Gabrielle aged 5 years and 7 months

Betty
★★★★★ **A soon to be classic!**
Reviewed in the United Kingdom on 4 February 2021
This is one of the most beautiful stories I've read in years. I'm pretty sure I enjoyed it more than my daughter who absolutely adored it. We both wish we had our own Moley. It evokes the charm and delight of Enid Blyton and Jane Austen.

Gemma Owen

☆☆☆☆☆ **Fantastic book**
Reviewed in the United Kingdom on 10 October 2021
Verified Purchase

This is a lovely book, I love the fact the mums job is a psychologist. The first children's book with a psychologist in a female role, really good for the field. The actual story is fantastic too. It was a story I read to my children but good for older children to read themselves too!

My favourite character was Moley because he was funny and helped people when he could. The best part of the book was when Moley and Owlie were arguing about whose fault it was, each blaming themselves, and they were told to stop - which was hilarious. If you make another book, I would like to see what happened on the holiday.

Rhys, 10 years old

I loved it!
I liked to look at the pictures while my mummy read the story. I loved all the characters but my favourite was Alexis because she is a good mummy. It was funny when Moley saw his own reflection and got angry at himself. I liked the bit where Moley was chosen to go on holiday. I would like to join Moley on another adventure.

Skye, 5 years old

Amazon Customer

★★★★★ **A delightful story!**
Reviewed in the United Kingdom on 14 February 2021
Verified Purchase

What a lovely story! Beautifully written and heartwarming. I particularly love the care and respirar the author shows for her audience. She doesn't talk down at children or simplify words but embellishes her sentences with wonderfully educational and descriptive words. Such a delight to read at bed time, we're anticipating each new chapter!

I am convinced it will become a children's classic.

Cass Grafton, Author

Draw your favourite characters, write your own review AND send it to Moley!

Moley's email: amolelikenoother@gmail.com

Thank you and well done!

140

Acknowledgements

I would like to express my heartfelt gratitude to:

Susannah Waters for being my editor and critic. I think I wouldn't have dared to even start this journey without meeting Susannah.

Monica Dailey Kauffman and her young students for being Moley's first enthusiastic readers and reviewers. Your love of the story and encouragement gave me wings and helped me to continue this adventure – both for my characters and myself!

Alison Larkin for her amazing *Just Do It* inspirational speech over some delicious Thai curry AND for making the most amazing recording of *A Mole Like No Other* audiobook. Moley and I are delighted and truly humbled that you've decided to work with us!

Rob and Renee English for being true Moley's Champions and also for allowing me to use the name of their beautiful little tortoise – Shelly.

Cassandra Grafton, for listening patiently, reading carefully, encouraging gently and supporting firmly.

Elena Tarnovskaya for remaining Moley's friend and helping me with the cover in the most reassuring and confidence–inducing manner. Again!

Carol Wellart for being an amazing artist, for listening carefully and working tirelessly until every single detail is right. Working with you is always such a pleasure!

My son, Sasha, for choosing Moley at a school Fair in the first place; and for typing up the book, because his old-fashioned Mother (me!) still writes long-hand. You are a star, my darling!

And last, but never least, **my husband Paul**, for reading and re-reading the book again and again, and rooting for Moley and me – ALWAYS.

Thank You!

About the Author

Julia B. Grantham lives in the South of England with her husband, son, two cats, Moley, Owlie, Shelly and all the other toys that make their appearance in her books: with ducks and pigeons in the garden, chickens across the road, as well as rabbits, squirrels, pheasants and deer, who visit often and hope also to make it into a book one day. Julia is a doctor and a training consultant, but books are her passion. She is a Harry Potter fanatic, an Ambassador for the *Jane Austen Literacy Foundation*, a writer and illustrator of Jane Austen-inspired travel fiction, and an author of two books for children.

Julia's Facebook profile: Search for **J.B. Grantham**

Direct Link: https://www.facebook.com/J.B.Grantham.Author/

Amazon Author's Page:

https://www.amazon.co.uk/stores/Julia-B.-Grantham/author/B08TMPBGDC

About the Illustrator

Carol Wellart is an award-winning artist and book illustrator from Czechia. She's a co-author of the first illustrated wolf chronicle *'Wolves are coming'* and her work was published in American magazines such as the *Spirituality & Health Magazine, International Wolf,* and *The Orion.*

Carol prefers creating images with themes of wildlife, nature, and literary characters, so when Julia and Carol joined forces to create the visuals for this book it was a union of kindred spirits!

Carol's Website:

https://carolwellart.com/artist

Printed in Great Britain
by Amazon